AT A

C000296925

GRAHAM ROY ORPIN

MERTIS B. HEIMBACH

AT ANY COST

The Story of
GRAHAM ROY ORPIN

LONDON
OVERSEAS MISSIONARY FELLOWSHIP
AGENTS: LUTTERWORTH PRESS

© C.I.M. OVERSEAS MISSIONARY FELLOWSHIP

First published	..	October 1964
Reprinted ..	..	November 1964
Reprinted ..	..	December 1964
Reprinted ..	..	July 1965
Reprinted ..	..	March 1966
Reprinted ..	..	September 1967
Reprinted ..	..	October 1968

S.B N 85363 000 3

Made in Great Britain

Published by Overseas Missionary Fellowship,
Newington Green, London, N.16,
and printed by The Camelot Press Ltd.,
London and Southampton

Trade Agents: The Lutterworth Press,
4 Bouverie Street, London E.C.4

CONTENTS

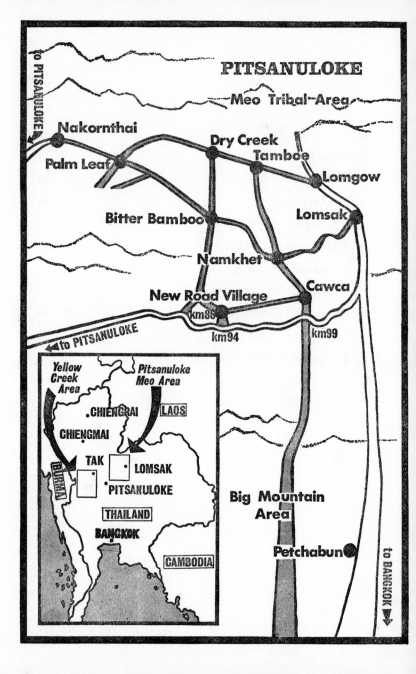

CHAPTER ONE

HIS TO LEAD

IN response to her request, Roy Orpin flipped through Gillian's hymnbook, autographed his favourite hymn and read aloud:

"My goal is God Himself, not joy, nor peace,
    Not even blessing, but Himself, my God;
'Tis His to lead me there—not mine, but His—
    At any cost, dear Lord, by any road."

"That's meant a lot to me ever since the Lord spoke to me at Easter camp."

"How *did* He speak to you?" queried Gillian.

"Through this hymn eventually," he answered. "Mum and Dad were true Christians and prayed for all of us kids, and I accepted the Lord as Saviour when I was quite young—but I didn't realize that to follow Him would mean surrendering my ambition. Oh, but it's a long story . . ." He broke off and handed the book back.

But this glimpse into his background had aroused Gillian's curiosity, and now that the other members of the committee had dispersed after the weekly session to arrange music for the open-air meetings, she persisted: "Go on, tell me."

"Well, I always wanted to be a farmer. I loved the land, and all that grows in it. My schooling and hobbies were all geared to this, and just when everything seemed set to go ahead, there suddenly came the challenge of the mission field. It was a real battle, I can tell you," he confessed. " 'Lord, send my brothers; send my sister; I'm not adequate, they are,' I prayed. But I couldn't get away from it somehow, and I lost all peace of mind.

"Then, at an Easter camp, I knew God was speaking to me. It was while we were singing this hymn that I yielded.

" 'Tis His to lead me there—not mine, but His—
At any cost, dear Lord, by any road."

He paused for a moment, then looked at her and smiled.

"It was all right after that," he said. "Peace flooded back, and I applied to come here to Bible School. Quite a change-over, though, from being a farmer to being a missionary!"

"It all goes to show that God doesn't call us because we are fitted for the job," observed Gillian. "He calls us first, and fits us as we obey Him, doesn't He?"

"Yes. And about that time He gave me a verse that settled my doubts and feelings of inadequacy," added Roy. "It was Philippians 4.13: 'I can do all things through Christ which strengtheneth me.' It's great to face the future with that."

Roy Orpin and Gillian Eland-Stewart were both in their final year at the New Zealand Bible Training Institute—B.T.I. as they affectionately called it. It was in downtown Auckland, and had been founded by Joseph Kemp whose love for Christ was kindled during the Welsh revival. Roy was from Otahuhu, a suburb of Auckland, and Gillian was a trained nurse from England. Serving on the music committee had thrown them together more than was usual in B.T.I., where men and girls were not permitted to go about together and any attachments were discouraged. This did not trouble Roy at all—indeed, he appreciated the principle behind this rule, for he did not want any distraction to hinder his preparation for the Lord's service. In any case, Gillian was English and he had no desire to marry an English girl! He admired her; her radiance as a Christian and her missionary enthusiasm attracted him, but this was all.

Even in Bible School, however, girls inevitably became a topic of discussion in leisure moments. One evening, the men gathered in Roy's room, knowing his attitude towards the fair sex, began to prod him:

"Why don't you have a bit of fun with the girls, Roy?" one asked. "You've never had a girl."

"I know, and I've been ragged about it enough," Roy retorted, "but personally, I don't believe that flirting is consistent with life in the fullness of the Spirit."

"But surely, there's nothing wrong with a mild flirtation, is there?"

"Well, it depends what you mean by that. I believe," said Roy with conviction, "that a fellow should keep himself unsullied for the life-partner God chooses for him."

No more was said, because the others respected his views. But they also knew that his attitude towards members of the staff revealed a less serious side of his nature, notably where Matron was concerned—a role he delighted to portray in skits on the staff.

At the end of one term, he and Ian gladly agreed to paint her bathroom floor, but her strict injunction not to get any paint on the bath set Roy musing—"So she doesn't want any paint on her bath . . ."

Leaving Ian to carry on, he dashed upstairs and soon dashed back again, flourishing something.

"I'm sure she won't mind *poster* paint on her bath!"

After a few deft strokes he resumed industriously painting the floor to an accompaniment of ensuing guffaws and comments:

"That seaweed sure does look real, doesn't it?"

"And what do you know! Little feet have been walking along the edge!"

Sudden silence followed the last remark as the commentators looked up into the astonished face of Matron. As Ian remarked after her withdrawal:

"For some strange reason she doesn't seem to appreciate the decoration of her bath—too bad to have to wipe off such artistic décor."

Roy and Ian had become close friends through their work together in children's meetings and had learned to value regular fellowship in prayer. One evening early in June, 1958, Roy knocked on Ian's door.

"Ian," he said as he strolled in, dropped down on the bed and leaned back against the wall, "my family's been interested in the China Inland Mission for a long time. I've got one aunt who has prayed for the C.I.M. for nearly thirty years. When Mr. Hogarth first went to China she prayed for him, and followed him all through. You remember Mr. Hogarth, I expect—pastor in my church in Otahuhu for a time?"

"Yes, I remember Mr. Hogarth. Last year we all went down to see him off to Malaya."

"It's that time that sticks in my mind, Ian. Just before the ship pulled away, he called out to me. 'We'll see you in Malaya some time!' I wondered, then, if the day would ever come when I would be sailing to some mission field. I know, now, that God wants me for His work somewhere. But I don't want to be led to the field just because of a personal interest in the C.I.M. I must be absolutely sure that this is the *Lord's* leading."

"God won't leave you in doubt, Roy. We both know that. Let's pray together about this," suggested Ian. . . .

A few days later, Roy enthusiastically beat a rat-a-tat on Ian's door again, stuck his head inside the room and called out: "I did it! I sent in my application papers to the C.I.M."

"Good-o!" Ian exclaimed.

In July it was Roy's turn to give the final appeal at the open air meeting. Mr. Deane, the Principal, had been giving lectures on the death of Christ. "One of these days you'll hear that John Deane has died," he said. "*Don't you believe it! I'll be more alive then than I ever was before.*"[1]

This calm assurance concerning death had deeply stirred Roy. "How many who pass by during the open air meetings will be there next week?" he asked himself. "How many of them can face death victoriously?" He was burdened for the crowds of heedless people he watched on open air nights, and he felt a special responsibility for this night. After a final review of his message, he stepped over to Ian's room.

"Ian, I know I'm not a preacher. I'm sure people can hear my knees knocking together when I get up to speak! But I feel so burdened for the people out there. I wonder when their last chance to turn to Christ will come. Let's pray that I'll be able to

[1] D. L. Moody is reported first to have said this.

get the message across. I do find it much easier speaking to children."

After brief but fervent prayer, Roy and Ian put on their red ties and slipped into their blue blazers to join the other hundred or more students who were gathering on the steps of the Baptist Tabernacle next door to the Institute. Others from the Baptist College nearby joined them. The church was at the top of Queen Street, which sloped steeply down to the docks. Roy felt the cold, damp breeze and buttoned his blazer. July, being midwinter in New Zealand, could be cold. It was a late shopping night and crowds of people moved past the church, intent on their purchases. Across the street stood another church, with a large neon sign flashing on and off: JESUS SAVES.

The conductor mounted the platform and the singing began. Roy usually brought his accordion along and with others accompanied the singing. But tonight he wanted to keep his mind on his message. Someone gave a testimony, followed by special music, and then it was time for Roy to speak. Cold perspiration trickled down his back. "I can do all things through Christ which strengtheneth me," he reminded himself, as he took his place.

"A man of wealth lay dying," he began. "As the family stood round, he said, 'I want my wife to have the home and the estate. . . .' His little daughter hearing this, exclaimed: 'Why, Papa, have you got a home where you're going?' Right from the time of our childhood, there is something in us which compels us to believe there is more to life than a few short years—then death—finished! The greater part of the human race, whether civilized or uncivilized, believes in some kind of hereafter.

"We see our friends and loved ones passing into a world unknown," he continued. "But God does not leave us in the dark as to that unknown. From the Bible we learn that our souls possess certain attributes . . . the real us. This will live on after our body is dead and lies in the grave. Jesus throws light upon this Eternity. He says, 'I am the resurrection, and the life: he that believeth in me, though he were dead, yet shall he live.' For those who trust Him, it will be the immediate entrance into the presence of the Father. He *is* Father to those who know Him. We are not afraid, even though we do not want to die. Death is not the grim reaper for us. It is not the Christian's greatest enemy. *It is his going Home.*"

He closed with a moving appeal, through contrasting the death of an infidel. "Is there anyone who will believe on Him tonight?" He waited, but there was no response from the crowd.

Roy walked off alone to think. The final hymn was being sung, but he could not stay. He *had* to get away. Why had there been no response? Were these people hardened to the message? Had they heard the Gospel too often? He looked round at the large churches; at the sign flashing, JESUS SAVES. His mind went back to his early days at B.T.I. Edna McLaren, a missionary of the C.I.M. tribal field in North Thailand, had shown her slides. He had never forgotten the last slide; one of an old heathen man. So many out there were growing old, and still had never even heard the Name of Christ. How could he stay here in New Zealand where on any street corner one could hear of Him?

But he could not think of the mission field without thinking of Gillian. He had known for some time that he not only admired her but that she was occupying his thoughts more and more. Gradually, it had dawned on him how much he really did care for her. He had not wanted to. He wanted nothing to deflect him from his studies, or from following the Lord with his whole heart and mind. True, Gillian already had applied to the C.I.M. The Lord was evidently leading them in the same direction.

Troubled and burdened, he walked on. And there, just ahead of him, he saw one of Gillian's close friends. He stopped, undecided. At that moment, she turned her head and saw him.

"Hello, Roy," she called. He hurried to catch up with her.

Somehow this seemed to be a sign. He had not intended talking of Gillian, but found himself doing so.

"She'd never like me, I know," he ended lamely. "But I just couldn't keep it."

"Don't worry so much, Roy," Gillian's friend replied, a gleam of amusement in her eyes. "I happen to know that Gill feels the same about you!"

Roy's astonishment was almost ludicrous. He could scarcely believe his ears. But his heart suddenly seemed to be floating on air!

CHAPTER TWO

FAITH BOUNDS FORWARD

ROY alternated between elation and concern in the hours that followed. He knew without question that he loved Gillian. Now there was this tremendous discovery that she might care for him. But he must know that this was of God and not of his own heart's choosing. Marriage was a serious matter for one who had covenanted with God to follow Him at any cost. There were none of the usual barriers others had experienced in beginning attachments. Gillian was a radiant Christian; she was wholly yielded to His service. The Lord was leading her to the mission field; even into the same Mission. But were these all straws he was all too eager to grasp?

"Lord, I want Thy will alone," he prayed simply before he slept. "Help me to know without a shadow of doubt whether Gill is Thy choice for me."

The answer came one day in Sermon Clinic Class. The second-year students gathered in the dining-room for this class and it was Gillian's turn to give the message that morning. Roy watched her walk to the end of the room and step up on the narrow platform. A ray of the late morning sun touched her golden hair as she turned to the class. Outside, a car horn sounded and the noise of the street traffic swelled. But her voice rose strong and clear as she began.

" 'For I am now ready to be offered, and the time of my

departure is at hand. I have fought a good fight. . . . Henceforth there is laid up for me a crown of righteousness, which the Lord, the righteous judge, shall give me at that day: and not to me only, but unto all them also that love his appearing.'

"What was Paul ready for?" she asked, her eyes glowing with deep earnestness. "He was ready to be offered as a sacrifice upon the altar. Paul's life had been a fight, well worthwhile. It called for the best in a man. His Lord was worthy of the very best that he could give. It had been a fight against all that Satan could devise to frustrate Paul in his service for God. And so it will be for us.

"Last week I was reading again *The Triumph of John and Betty Stam*. Only three years out of Bible School, at the beginning of their missionary service, God held out to them martyrs' crowns. Their course was ended and they were ready to be offered.

"I've been thinking, too, of the five young men who died for Christ in Ecuador. One of them wrote while still in college: 'He is no fool who gives what he cannot keep to gain what he cannot lose.'[1]

"All these young people were the same age, or a few years older, than we who are here today. We do not know how long the course is that God has prepared for us, or how soon we shall come to the end. The length does not matter. It is how we run the race that counts."

Roy sat stilled by the message. This was just how he felt. He went on listening, with a sense of exultation crowding through him, as Gillian's clear voice read verses[2] quoted years before by John C. Stam.

> Afraid? Of what?
> To feel the spirit's glad release?
> To pass from pain to perfect peace,
> The strife and strain of life to cease?
> Afraid—of that?

[1] *Shadow of the Almighty* by Elizabeth Elliott, p.15.
[2] By E. H. Hamilton.

Afraid? Of what?
Afraid to see the Saviour's face?
To hear His welcome, and to trace
The glory gleam from wounds of grace?
 Afraid—of that?

Afraid? Of what?
A flash, a crash, a piercèd heart;
Darkness, light, O Heaven's art!
A wound of His a counterpart!
 Afraid—of that?

Afraid? Of what?
To do by death what life could not—
Baptize with blood a stony plot,
Till souls shall blossom from the spot?
 Afraid—of that?

The final hymn, *The sands of time are sinking*, was being sung, but Roy's mind was caught in the impact of the blazing revelation of God's answer to his prayer. This was the girl he wanted on the mission field. There was no shadow of doubt. He knew. *Gillian was God's choice for him.*

Slowly he became conscious of his immediate surroundings, and the words of the hymn the others were singing: "The bride eyes not her garment, but her dear bridegroom's face." He glanced at Gillian. Their eyes met, and his face flushed a deep red. He was sure others had noticed. It was painful, this trying to keep from showing her that he loved her. Would he have strength for this for the remainder of the school year? Swiftly, the verse the Lord had given him earlier, and which had been his source of strength so many times, flooded his heart: "I can do all things through Christ which strengtheneth me." He could wait, now that he knew God's will in this.

But with this assurance there came the consciousness of another problem. In his application to the C.I.M. he had written, "No attachment". This was now incorrect. What should he do? He would have to let the Mission know, but would it make a difference? He went first to a member of the Institute Staff, and then to see Mr. Michell, Home Director of the C.I.M. in New Zealand.

Seated in Mr. Michell's office, Roy began: "Since I sent in my application to the Mission a few months ago, I have discovered that one statement I made concerning a heart attachment has now become incorrect. I am troubled about this as I don't know what effect it will have if I alter it."

"Is she interested in the Mission?" Mr. Michell asked quickly.

"O yes! She has already been accepted for the Candidates' Course next January, in fact! There is no understanding between us," he hastened to explain, "and I don't like to bandy her name about, but she is Gillian Eland-Stewart."

Mr. Michell's face cleared. "I appreciate your coming like this, Roy. And I am sure it will be understood that you acted in all honesty in your first application, and now your answer must be altered. You know, of course, that each of you will be considered individually and you must be prepared for the fact that one could be accepted and the other not?"

"Yes," Roy answered quietly. "But I know I can speak for Gill, too, when I say that we want only God's will for our lives and service."

Graduation came in December and with it the reward of patient waiting. At last he could talk freely with Gillian of all the Lord's dealings in the last few months; learn how God had met with her in those last months in Bible School as she had realized her own heart's choosing and wonderment as she believed Roy cared, too. Roy took Gillian to visit his family, and in January they met again at the C.I.M. in Auckland for the six weeks' Candidates' Course. There were four others: one fellow and three girls, all of whom had been together at B.T.I. The days of Candidates' Course sped quickly by in happy fellowship.

One evening in March, the silence of the Orpin home was shattered by the banging of a car door and the sound of running feet at the back door. In rushed Roy and flung his arms around his mother.

"Mum! Dad! Your son is going to be a missionary and maybe leave his bones in some foreign country!" Then he continued more quietly, "I've been accepted by the C.I.M.! We had our interviews with the Council members, and all six of us have been accepted. Gill and the others will be sailing for Singapore soon, but I am to stay home for another year to get practical experience in church work."

"Praise the Lord!" Mr. Orpin exclaimed.

"Our prayers have been answered," Roy's mother said. "And not only ours, but your grandmother's as well. She longed that her son would be a minister, but God has answered through you!"

Soon after their acceptance by the Mission, Roy and Gillian announced their engagement. They had agreed to the suggestion that Roy remain at home a further year for practical training. But Mr. Michell was not happy about their sailing separately. One evening he called the two of them into his office.

"I must write to Singapore tomorrow to let Headquarters know how many will be sailing from New Zealand to enter the Language Centre there. But I have no assurance as to what the Lord's will is concerning you, Roy. I think the three of us should have prayer together about it." A quiet sense of peace settled over Roy as they knelt in prayer. His Lord, who had led each step till now, knew the way ahead. He would reveal His will in His time.

The following morning, Mr. Michell called them in again. His face was beaming. "I am no longer in doubt, for the Lord has clearly spoken to me. Here's the verse I was given this morning: 'Let my people go that they may serve me.'"

So they sailed together.

It was early morning, April 23, 1959, when their ship approached the lovely island of Singapore. Roy and Gillian watched excitedly as the mauve-tinted mound set in an emerald sea, turned into land that looked a veritable tropical paradise. Their ship moved into harbour—largest in Southeast Asia, Roy remembered—among ships of all nations anchored in its waters.

They were surprised to see so many down to meet them; Mission Directors and staff, and the group of new workers from South Africa who had arrived in Singapore ahead of them.

Soon they were in the Mission van driving through the city to their new home in the Language Centre in Chancery Lane. Roy was intent on all he saw; the busy modern city streets, flanked with beautiful trees and flowering shrubs; cars, cyclists and pedestrians vying for position in the lanes. All the races of Singapore seemed to be represented: Chinese, Malays, people from India and Europe. This was Singapore, dynamic mixture of East and West! He wondered if one could ever tire of all that was new and colourful and exciting here.

"Have you heard about Lilian Hamer?" one of the new workers from South Africa asked quietly.

"No, what's that?"

"She was shot and killed on April 18, as she was coming down from a Lisu village."

"Lilian Hamer . . . shot!" Roy exclaimed. "Why, she was a fellow-worker of Edna McLaren's who showed us slides of the tribal work in North Thailand while we were in Bible School!"

"Yes, that's right. She'd just moved into a little shack in a Lisu village in the mountains. We even heard that Edna was up for a visit only a few weeks before. Lilian was on her way down to market to get supplies. No one knows why she was shot. She was left to die on the trail. Mr. Crane, who went to see about her funeral, said it could happen to anyone on those North Thailand trails where there is so much robbery and violence."

The kaleidoscope of colour that was Singapore to a new arrival, seemed to fade as Roy came thus starkly face to face with the cost of discipleship; the cost of this life to the small band of missionaries in North Thailand and the Mission as a whole.

CHAPTER THREE

THE LANGUAGE HURDLE

ROY found the Language Centre a melting-pot in itself, with the several nationalities represented among the new workers. Those from New Zealand and South Africa were soon joined by a large party from North America, and another from

England, including a few Swiss and Germans. Altogether, there were now forty-one new workers for the C.I.M.'s overseas work in Southeast Asia.

"It's certainly strange hearing all the different accents," Roy said to Gillian, "and especially to find out that *I* have an accent, too!" he laughed.

"My room-mate is Natalie Ray, a nurse from the U.S.A.," Gillian replied. "I didn't know I had an accent until she kept asking me to repeat words so that she could understand what I was saying! But isn't it interesting to learn how other people live and think and to know that God has called us all together here to learn and prepare to serve Him somewhere in these lands!"

Soon the exciting day—D-Day—arrived, when each of the forty-one new workers was designated to his future field of missionary service.

Gillian came running over to Roy as she came from the final meeting with the Directors. "It's wonderful to have it all settled, isn't it? Were you surprised when North Thailand was first suggested to us?"

"No, I can't say that I was," Roy answered slowly. "The morning after we arrived I was thinking so much about Lilian Hamer. I woke early and was reading II Corinthians 5, when the Lord spoke to me in verse 9: 'Wherefore we labour, that, whether present or absent, we may be accepted of him.' I realized then that it didn't matter whether our term of service is long or short, if we are accepted of Him. I told the Lord then that I was willing to go to North Thailand, if He should lead. But I didn't tell you about that, then, Gill. I was afraid of influencing in any way our thinking about such an important matter. It had to be all of Him, and I have assurance that it is."

"I, too," Gillian agreed quietly.

The five months of initial language study and orientation in Singapore were soon over and the workers began to scatter to the various designated countries. Roy and Gillian travelled as far as Bangkok together; from there Roy continued on to Chiengrai to the language centre for young men. Gillian joined young women workers in Tak, 200 miles south of Chiengrai. They would meet again at Field Conference time, and at Christmas.

Meanwhile, they each had covenanted to let nothing interfere with their studies, looking forward to the day when, the required Thai study completed, they could turn together to one of the tribal languages. For there was yet another designation ahead of them.

Thailand was quite different from Singapore. The country villages and people seemed more primitive in comparison to the busy, modern seaport. But the loveliness of the Thai countryside was a continual joy to Roy. He loved beauty. He had arrived at the end of the rainy season, when a delightful fresh greenness touched the whole land.

"Chiengrai lies nestled at the base of two great mountain ranges," he wrote home. "The one to the west runs north into Burma, while the eastern range loses itself in Laos. It is rather awesome to see these heavily wooded mountains rising steeply from the plains with their rich, heavy heads of ripened grain. These hills shelter tiger, leopard, monkey, and many other types of wild life. But it is in these hills that our interest lies, for scores of tribal villages are scattered throughout them."

It was not long before Roy had an opportunity to visit those mountains. Neville Long, who was in charge of the language students, asked him one day: "Would you like a trip up to the tribes?"

Roy's eyes lighted with eagerness. "*Would* I? When can we go?"

"This week-end. We will be visiting Peter and Jean Nightingale, and on Sunday Peter will take you up to Ka Yeh, the Akha village where the only Akha Christians in Thailand live."

It was a unique experience for Roy to walk into Peter and Jean Nightingale's little house in the Northern Thai village of Nambokhaw. He stood and looked round at the rough bamboo walls and then up to the grass roof. He said nothing, but wondered if he could ever get used to such rough living.

At that moment a child began to cry from the next room, and Roy went in to comfort him. He had a way with children, because he loved them, and soon he and little Andrew were sitting together on the floor building a castle with the blocks lying about. Peter and Jean had gone to round up the other two children who were playing in the village. When they returned, some of the Christian boys from the Nambokhaw church came, too, to see the new "reverend". Roy was a bit startled when, after the initial introductions, he was left alone with them. To his relief they sat down around the scattered blocks, and his long silences while trying to think through further Thai phrases were made easier and less obvious as together they sought the pieces to finish off the project under construction.

On Sunday, Roy hiked up with Peter to Ka Yeh Akha village. It was an exhilarating climb through beautiful country-side; the morning was perfect and the views magnificent. At the approach to the village they halted before a tall gateway, built squarely of wood, festooned with demon screens, crudely carved wooden figures and phallic symbols to ensure the fertility of the villagers.

"What's that draped on the top of the gate?" Roy asked.

"That's the remains of the dog sacrificed to keep away the evil spirits," Peter said calmly.

Roy shuddered, his thoughts too deep to frame a reply. But snarling, angry dogs rushing from the various small bamboo shanties as they went through the gateway, quickly took his mind from the dead dog. They picked their way between snuff-ling pigs, clucking hens, goats, yelping dogs and Akha children. And then they were face to face with Ya Ju and his wife, Me Chu, who greeted them warmly and invited them into their home. Roy's revulsion at the village entrance was quickly forgotten as he looked into the bright faces of these two for whom he had prayed ever since he had heard of their coming from Burma to help the white missionary preach to their own people. Ya Ju with his jaunty sailor-like cap and bell-bottom trousers looked just like the pictures he had seen of Akha men, while Me Chu seemed to be wearing most of her wardrobe on her head as he had heard Akha women described. The conical cap from which hung rows of chains, beads, silver coins, and decorated with monkey fur and red pom-poms, was much more elaborate than was the tiny beaded black bolero jacket and short scanty skirt that completed her costume.

Roy had brought his piano accordion along with him and what

a happy time they had in the worship service together. Me Chu sat on the edge of the bed platform nursing her five-day-old baby as they sang. In the prayer-time following, Ya Ju poured out his heart to the Lord: "O Lord, you know all about my troubles. You know I've lost all my pepper crop and all my rice; how my house was even set on fire. But I thank You for Your help in spite of it all. Help me to witness to my neighbours and win them to You."

Roy could not understand the words, but he felt moved as he heard this Akha man praying so fervently. On their way down the mountain, Peter interpreted the prayer to Roy and they talked together of what it must mean to these two young Christians to live far from their own home in the midst of people so deeply bound in demon-worship and immorality, looked down upon by all the other tribes as degraded. How often their thoughts must turn to their home in Burma where there were other Christian Akha; where there would be love and understanding instead of the persecution and hate they had endured here. And yet here they stayed, pin-points of light in such gross darkness.

"For a long time these people have been just names," Roy wrote to the Superintendent, "but now they are real persons needing prayer and help to stand. . . . The simplicity of these mountain folk attracts me. The tremendous possibilities that lie behind young lads my own age challenge me!"

In the weeks that followed, Roy had the opportunity of trekking to a Yao and a Lisu village. Back at the Chiengrai home he shared his experiences with the others. "I enjoyed every minute of it. In the woods there were butterflies of rarest species, and when we got to the Yao village we were told that a tiger had walked the same trail just half an hour before us! But best of all, of course, was meeting the people, seeing them where they live, being challenged to pray for individuals!"

"What are your impressions of the tribes after these trips?" Neville asked.

"Well . . . the Akha left me with the impression of a darkened, degraded, grubby and needy people. The Yao; lovable, handsome and intelligent. The Lisu; proud, yet somehow decidedly attractive. And the little I did see of the Lahu, a people in bond-age needing what only the Gospel can give them."

"Have you any definite leading to any one tribe yet?" one of the others asked.

"No-o-o, not yet. The first impulse is to wish one could divide up and remain with them all! I confess I am attracted to one particular tribe, but I'm not sure enough about it yet."

With his appetite thus whetted for the hills, Roy was the more determined to get a good grasp of the Thai language before entering tribal work. He and Gillian had disciplined themselves to one letter a week, when it would have been easy to have written daily with so much to share. But constant application to language study can become a weary grind, and Roy was finding it so. One morning at breakfast he said, "The last four nights in a row I've been going over Thai phrases all night. Some sounds just refuse to come right, and the effort to sort out idioms leaves me tired and confused."

"I know how you feel," said one of the fellows, who was a few months ahead of Roy in Thai study. "The teacher just will not excuse a sound that is not correct. He's a good teacher, of course, but he is not very encouraging. Yesterday he told me I would never learn to speak Thai; that I was hopeless. So helpful!"

"It really is frustrating, after studying several months, still to find it difficult to say much. I know I'm too tense at it, but it is hard to relax."

"We have a badminton set here," suggested one, "but there really isn't time to get in a good game before supper."

"Why not knock off study at 4.30 instead of 5?" suggested Neville. "I'm sure the young people from the local church or the Christian school would enjoy playing with you. And here's another suggestion for you, Roy," he continued. "Why don't you try to find a suitable place to spend week-ends with the Thai? Mr. Tong Dee may have some suggestions."

That very afternoon three of them went to see Mr. Tong Dee, the headmaster of the Christian school. On the way they passed a large ornate temple whose extensive grounds were filled with thousands of worshippers as this was a special occasion when new robes were presented to the priests. They stood and watched while hundreds of saffron-robed priests filed out of the temple, past the kneeling worshippers. Gifts were offered them from beautiful silver bowls, and as the priests' baskets filled they were emptied into waiting ox-carts. Quick to use such an opportunity, the young missionaries soon had distributed several hundred tracts to the people, who took them readily.

At the Christian school they were met by the pretty wife of the headmaster, with the ever-ready glass of *nam som*, an orange soft drink, and soon Mr. Tong Dee himself came in. Christian fellowship with these folk was always rich. The first Thai Church in Chiengrai had been organized by one of the American Presbyterian Mission pioneers in 1890. When the new church building was completed in 1915, a history of the church was deposited in the corner stone, with these words: "Truly this has been a mother of churches." And so it was that many smaller groups of believers, like those in Nambokhaw, could be found about the plain. And the C.I.M. Overseas Missionary Fellowship, coming into North Thailand in response to the needs of the tribes, had received encouragement and help from the Thai Christians.

The outcome of Roy's visit to Mr. Tong Dee, who was more than ready to help in any way he could, was a suggestion he contact two young teachers living by themselves on the school grounds. "I'll approach them, if you like, and let you know how they feel about it," he offered. "You could help them with their English while they helped you with Thai. These two men are not Christians, but it would be an excellent opportunity for you."

"And we would like to invite anyone to come over to our place to play badminton any afternoon at 4.30," Roy added before they left.

The next afternoon two young Thai teachers arrived to play badminton. One was named Jumrut. In the course of the afternoon, they got into a lively discussion.

"But you missionaries don't seem to be like the movie stars! You don't fit into what we imagined foreigners to be like. You don't smoke and drink and run around with women like the people we see in the films. What makes you so different?"

This was the opening Roy had prayed for, scarcely dreaming it would come so soon. In a moment he was telling how he had come to know Christ as his Saviour and what point and purpose it had given to his life, even to coming to North Thailand to tell others the Good News. When they left, Jumrut warmly invited Roy to spend week-ends with him at the Christian school.

Every Saturday thereafter Roy went over to the school and spent the night there, coming home on Sunday after church. He found that Jumrut was interested in the accordion, so took his along and gave him lessons. One evening Jumrut opened up. "I see many Christians," he said in his slow, imperfect English. "They not as good as me. I think they all hypocrites. That is why I do not want to become Christian. But you are not the same. If everyone like you, perhaps I like Christianity. You read Bible every morning, every evening. You always on time and well disciplined. You always want to talk about Jesus. He must mean much to you. You had wonderful life on farm in New Zealand, but come to Thailand to tell us of Jesus. I do not understand that."

Roy wrote to his parents about Jumrut. "The situation at the school is sometimes a puzzle as to its worth as far as language study is concerned. But Jumrut is showing increasing interest in the Gospel and often comes to read portions of the Thai Bible with me. Sometimes he says: 'This is almost the same as Buddhism.' But in spite of such remarks, he is eager to come to church and talk about the Gospel with me. I feel very limited in what I can say, and see how easy it is to feel frustrated with the language when there's a longing to say something, and I haven't the vocabulary. But I trust the Lord to speak through His Word. I do feel God has His purpose in this contact. *Do pray for Jumrut.*"

CHAPTER FOUR

A COMPLETE SURPRISE

"YOU can't speak Thai any better than when you came here six months ago!" Roy's Thai teacher exclaimed in exasperation one day in February. "You are trying to go too fast. You can never learn Thai that way. You are in a hurry to get into the hills like all the rest of them!"

Roy's heart sank. The teacher, he felt, had been unnecessarily scathing in his remarks; nevertheless, it was discouraging. He went upstairs to find Mrs. Crane. He could use a sympathetic ear, he thought, ruefully. Mr. and Mrs. Allan Crane had relieved the Neville Longs who had gone home on furlough. Just now Mr. Crane was away at Field Council meetings in Chiengmai where the tribal designations of several new workers who had arrived on the field earlier, were to be decided.

Roy found Mrs. Crane in the guest-room making the bed in preparation for Peter Nightingale who would be returning next day with Mr. Crane. "The teacher's told everybody off no matter how well they speak, but just the same, I know I still can't speak as I feel I ought. Oh, how I have to guard against frustration, and not expect these idioms to come overnight. I find I could so easily be provoked to anger. Please pray for me, Mrs. Crane, that my attitude will show the Master's grace."

Evelyn Crane, who knew well the demands of learning more than one language through the years of studying Chinese, Lisu and Thai, could understand. Then and there she prayed with him, and her encouragement helped.

Roy was in the garden at the front the next day when Allan Crane and Peter Nightingale came in. Allan Crane looked tired, but said he had taken the trip well. He had had a recent attack of angina. He handed Roy a letter from the Superintendent. But Roy was so interested in hearing news of the others' designations, he didn't open his own letter immediately. He was not expecting anything important. His and Gillian's tribal designations would probably not be settled for several months yet. When he did open the letter, he found it to be a joint letter to him and Gillian. As he read, he suddenly tensed. He had been wrong; their designations *had* been considered. "After much prayer and thought over the future of all our workers as yet undesignated," the Superintendent had written, "it was our united feeling that you and Gillian ought to make the *White Meo* your sphere of particular ministry. I want you prayerfully to consider this designation before the Lord, and then let me know as soon as possible how you feel about it."

Roy was stunned. "*White Meo!* Why, I've scarcely thought of that tribe!" He wondered how Gillian would feel; and it seemed suddenly significant that she must have thought of the Meo tribe, as she already had spent some time in Yellow Creek among the Blue Meo and, from all accounts, had lost her heart to them! He remembered how he had smiled at a paragraph in an earlier circular of Gill's, as she had described her home in Tak. "At the bottom of the garden is a wide river and beyond stretch the mountains. As I look out to them, I can imagine all the tribes hidden away there, and wonder which one of those mountains Roy and I will be climbing together, with the precious Gospel." He had smiled as he had thought: "Why is Gill so certain it may be *those* mountains we will be climbing together; why not some of *my* mountains here!" But her last sentence had stayed with him: "Pray that we may be sure of God's will as to where we eventually go."

They *had* prayed. Was this God's answer: *White Meo?* He couldn't deny the need. Their Field Superintendent, Mr. Carlson, had been suddenly called away on an early furlough because of family illness, and the only man who had a working knowledge of White Meo, Mr. Heimbach, had been appointed Acting Superintendent in his stead. This left only Miss Dorothy Jones to "man" the White Meo field.

"Am I the man You want for the White Meo?" he prayed quietly. And into the stillness of his heart, bowed before God, stole the consciousness of God's voice: "This is the way, walk ye in it. This way involves the Cross, but this is the way of greater faith."

Rising, he went over to the gramophone and the box of Gospel

Recordings records. He found the Meo record he had noticed earlier, wondering at the time why it was there, as he had not met any Meo in this area. Out of curiosity he put it on and played it through. This, then, would be the language they would be studying next!

"The words, White Meo, were, I confess, a complete surprise to me," he wrote to the Acting Superintendent some time later. "However, the initial surprise has given place to a sense of peace that the decision of the Council is the Lord's will for us. I haven't any doubts as to whether I'll manage village life, as I've always been used to back country life. I admit sometimes this business of mixing with school-teachers makes me want to teach a more simple people!" But tribal life was going to be specially hard for Roy, much harder than for many, because of his love of beauty and order.

Roy wrote also to his family and friends: "It was a strange feeling to know that we were finally appointed to what will be our life work, and that as yet I haven't even seen the people! Mr. Heimbach will be taking me to visit the Meo in the next couple of weeks. He has to return to his centre there to pack their belongings as they will be living in Chiengmai now.

"There are many Meo villages yet untouched by the Gospel, and the desperate need is for teaching those already in the faith. Of course, Gill will know them far better than I, as she has made several treks to them already. This trip will involve several hundred miles of travel before I get there. Some of the areas are quite inaccessible and take days of walking, so I'd better keep my walking legs in shape!"

With a pair of walking shoes, flask of water and a change of clothing, Roy was off to meet Ernie Heimbach on the train to Pitsanuloke. Then, fortified with a breakfast of curry and rice, they caught a bus which took them into some of the wildest and thickest jungle that Roy had ever seen. The air was fresh and cool as they stepped off the bus. "*Pai!*" called the driver and off it went leaving two solitary figures with packs on their backs in the middle of a green wilderness broken only by the ribbon of road.

After committing themselves and the trip into the Lord's hands, Ernie Heimbach swung off the road on to the Meo trail, with Roy full of wonder following behind. He loved the beauty of the jungle and the varied vegetation. The trail led through bamboo groves, and sometimes the gloom of the virgin forest enshrouded them. Ahead, the mountain rose to a height of 4,000 feet, and the packs began to weigh heavily on their backs as they climbed. But there was much to catch their attention—to keep their thoughts off aching backs. Gibbons scrambled across banana leaves; wild jungle fowl with gay plumage scuttled to cover while they stopped to watch. And there was the little Thai man with a home-made gun on his shoulder who escorted them past his none-too-friendly elephant.

The sun had lost its strength and was sinking beyond the distant ridges when they reached the last stream before the village.

"Let's have a bath and a change," suggested Ernie.

"Why do the Meo have their villages so high?" Roy asked, dropping down on a large boulder and easing his pack off his back.

"Because the climate is good for opium growing. All the Meo plant opium except a few of the Christians."

"Then why do they make their trails go over the *top* of all the hills rather than around the sides?"

"No one knows. That's just the way they do it!"

A delightful breeze sprang up as they entered a clearing in the jungle. This was Namkhet. Squat houses with rough-hewn walls and palm leaf roofs lay scattered about in no particular order. Numerous pigs, busily seeking a scavenger meal, roamed about freely.

"*Ooo oooo oooo ooo,*" yodelled a pretty Meo lass, and a dozen or so pigs rushed towards her as she began to fill a large trough with mash. Roy stopped to watch. The red wool tassels on her turban bobbed with every movement as she expertly warded off the neighbours' pigs. The beauty of the intricate embroidery of her red sash seemed a trifle incongruous with her menial task.

Entering one of the houses, as humble as the others, they were greeted by Dorothy Jones, who was soon pushing welcome cups of hot tea into their hands. Roy was grateful to be able to sit down, slip off his pack, and stretch his weary legs. But not for long. Soon he was helping Dorothy drag in another log to add to the fire in the centre of the earthen floor. The room began to fill with sturdy mountain people, the fire lighting their leathery features as they warmly greeted Ernie and the newcomer.

It was hard to believe that only five years before none of these people had ever heard the Name of Jesus. Eighteen-year-old Ying seemed to have a smile that nearly halved his face. It made Roy want to smile back even though he could not say a word in Meo. Ying, he learned, was the only believer in a large family, and had stood alone against much opposition. He was truly a gem, with a heart on fire for the Lord. Having been Ernie's right-hand man in the translation of the Gospel of John, he had a deep love for the Word of God.

That night Roy and Ernie slept in Mblia Dua's house. He was the oldest male believer among the Meo, and had broken with a thirty-year habit of opium smoking. His family had been the first to give up planting opium, but a spirit of covetousness for material things was spoiling his otherwise good testimony. He was also the father of Simon and Nzoe, two budding church leaders, and pretty Leah, the pampered daughter of the family.

Roy had scarcely gone to sleep on the mat spread on the hard floor, when the horses penned at the back of the house somehow broke loose. The commotion of catching them again had hardly quieted before work began for the day, with the steady thud-thud of the footmill pounding the rice. These Meo certainly are an energetic, hard-working people, he thought sleepily.

They were setting off for Palm Leaf village the next day when a group of smartly dressed young fellows asked to have their picture taken. Roy was astonished to see what dandies they were with their red embroidered sashes, dark glasses and some even painted with lipstick! "It's odd how they hang old tooth-brushes on their silver neck rings as if they were some precious possession," Roy commented as they swung off down the trail towards Palm Leaf, ten hours' hike away. Ying was with them this morning, leading the horse carrying the packs. But after only two hours on the trail, Ernie began to lag and it was soon evident he was feverish. They sat down to rest, but his fever mounted.

"I don't know what's wrong with me," he said. "But I don't think I can go any further. It may be malaria. Ying says he has a relative in Cliff Village near here. They aren't Christians, but perhaps they'll let us stay the night."

In the Meo house Roy dosed Ernie with all the pills they had with them. Then he suggested, "I'll go back and get Dorothy. She's a nurse and will know what to do." When he arrived back with Dorothy, he found Ernie stretched out on the floor on the family's only mattress, shivering under their red blanket. They had offered their very best to their guest.

That night Roy lay down beside Ernie with only a bamboo mat between him and the ground, wondering how he could take another night of it. His head throbbed and his stomach felt not too comfortable, either. He wondered what it was the folks had given him for supper, but the light was too poor for him to inspect it. He tried to sleep, but the little boy of the family kept chopping horse-feed just a few feet from his head. Every once in a while a piece flew over on to his blanket. Right above their heads hung the family's spirit shelf, with its sheet of paper smeared with chicken blood and feathers.

He turned over and tried to find a more comfortable position. There were certainly lots of sounds in the night; dogs barking, rats gnawing and other noises that set his imagination working. He wondered what it was that was breathing so heavily on the other side of the wall-boards near his head. Suddenly, there was a mad grunting, snorting and squealing.

"What's that, Ernie?" Roy called.

"Forget it," Ernie answered sleepily. "Just a pile of pigs sleeping on top of each other to keep warm. After a while the one on the bottom feels uncomfortable and wants to get out. Somewhat startling at midnight, though, isn't it?"

Ernie was feeling well enough by morning to start off slowly. This time it was to drop right down to the Kay River, and then climb again to 5,000 feet. It was a steep climb to make after a sleepless night. Roy's feet were hurting, too. When he got to the top of the ridge, he found that his feet were badly swollen, and walked uncomplainingly the rest of the way barefooted. Avoiding the village of Bitter Bamboo, they took the trail straight across the ridge. This brought them through some of the darkest, tangled jungle Roy had yet seen.

"What a wild and forsaken place!" he exclaimed.

"It is," Ernie agreed. "I often feel that a few feet off the trail here you would step on ground no human foot has ever touched since the world began. Makes you feel small, doesn't it?"

On a bit further, the trail squeezed between two massive boulders. "Notice this, Roy," Ernie called. "One of these rocks is called *The Dragon*, and the other *The Tiger*. See the pile of leaves at the side? Every traveller, Meo, Thai, or Chinese trader, who fears the spirits of the jungle adds a leaf to the pile as he passes by. They fear a horse or a man might otherwise break a leg or be killed." He scattered the pile with his foot as they moved on.

It was late afternoon when they caught sight of Palm Leaf. The chipped log seats of the little missionary home afforded a pleasant resting-place for weary bones. Walter Moody was in good spirits, having many evidences of the Lord's enabling during his long spell alone. He was a new worker from the Blue Meo side of the work, but had come to help temporarily during the shortage of workers on this side. He stirred up the log fire in the middle of the floor and soon had a welcome cup of coffee, and a hot rice meal for them.

Roy was feeling better now. He looked around at the rough board walls, and up at the palm leaf roof. The soot from the fire had darkened everything. The plastic curtains in the doorway to the bedroom looked grimy and dusty. On the home-made cupboards and shelves were layers of ashes, deposited by the open cooking fire just as in any tribal home. So this was the home of his senior missionary!

As evening drew on, a few of the Meo believers came in to talk. Doong Ye sat unsmiling by the fire on a low wooden stool. He had been the first believer in that village; a strong, forceful character who had braved the opposition of the village leaders and helped build this house so that missionaries could live here and teach them of the Lord. When the Heimbachs had left a few months before, he and two others had been baptized. He had been full of joy and, with costly victory, had broken with the dreaded drug that enslaved so many. Now he sat with a cold, indifferent attitude towards Ernie's earnest exhortations.

Sin had robbed him of his warm-hearted love for the Lord.

"It's sad to see Doong Ye, once the vigorous leader of the group here, so changed," Walter explained. "Both he and the other two men have gone back to opium planting, and on occasions I've even found them smoking the stuff. It seems the whole future of the Palm Leaf church lies in the balances."

As Roy lay down that night, he watched the flickering shadows which the low fire made on the roof above him. Next door the eerie clanging of spirit gongs and the rhythmic chanting of the *shaman* in animistic spirit worship went on without respite. Every now and then he could hear the *shaman* shake his spirit rattles and bark like a dog. It seemed to Roy that the enemy of souls was mocking all the efforts that had been made to establish a church in this place. He could even hear his incessant taunting: "You don't feel any call to the Meo! You've never had any definite leading! You never could love *these people*! What could *you* do in such a situation?"

The next day was taken up with packing the Heimbach household equipment. But after lunch, Ernie suggested they have a time to pray and discuss the needs of the Meo church and the work as a whole. "The need is for *revival*," he said. "Only God can bring the change we so desperately want. We have long felt the need of reinforcements in the White Meo work. The field is scattered, and with our present personnel we have hardly been able to hold our own. Walter here belongs to the Blue Meo; he'll be leaving Palm Leaf soon. With our going, only Dorothy Jones is left for the White Meo work. We hope Doris Whitelock, who will be transferring from Central Thailand, can come soon to be a companion to Dorothy, *but we need men*. We must do all we can to press on with the Gospel, *now*, for the time may be short. There yet remain areas of Meo that we have hardly touched, and some we have never reached. The need is for *enlargement* beyond our present spheres of witness. And then there's more Bible translation, and literature work, and more teaching to build up the Meo believers!"

"There's need all right," Walter said. "Your and Gillian's coming is a very definite answer to prayer."

Ernie then read from Isaiah 54.1-4: "Sing, O barren, thou that

c

didst not bear . . . Enlarge the place of thy tent . . . For thou shalt break forth on the right hand and on the left . . . Fear not . . . for thou shalt not be put to shame." Then they went to prayer, pouring out their hearts for the revival of these poor, weak, straying sheep, and for the turning of many heathen hearts to the Lord in the days ahead.

Down the mountain again, and across scorching barren plains, Roy and Ernie reached Pitsanuloke about dark. After getting cleaned up at a small hotel, they went to see about getting the Heimbach luggage to the railway station. Roy was beginning to feel civilized once again. The electric lights, flashing coloured neon signs, and modern equipment attractively displayed in the shop windows was a marked contrast to the rugged village life they had just left. "Why couldn't one be assigned to a place like this?" he asked jokingly.

Later, parting with Ernie on the train, Roy made his way by bus back to Chiengrai. What a welcome sight the big old Chiengrai house was!

Allan Crane was out in the front garden when Roy limped wearily in. "How was the trip?" he asked.

"Well, I'll have to nurse my blistered feet and catch up on a week's sleep, then I'll be all right," he replied.

Later he confided to Mr. Crane: "I guess I'm out of form, but that climb up to Namkhet nearly broke my back, not to mention the ordeal of sleepless nights and feeling sick most of the time. But to see Mr. Heimbach involved and so concerned with the condition of many of the Christians nearly broke my heart. Their obvious indifference to his exhortations left me with impressions not altogether favourable towards the people. I just feel weary and sick at heart over the whole trip. I wonder if I will ever make the grade?"

CHAPTER FIVE

A HELPMEET AND A HOME

"WHERE are all the Nightingales going to sleep?" was the the question going round the Chiengrai house. Mr. Crane, whose health had been far from good for some time, needed to conserve his strength for the translation of the Lisu Old Testament on which he and Mrs. Crane were working, so Peter and Jean Nightingale had been asked to help at the Chiengrai Language centre. But there were five Nightingales, too many for one bedroom.

"Why not divide my room on the porch for the two older children?" Roy suggested. "I don't need all that space for myself."

A few days later when Peter and Jean arrived they were surprised to find two beds in the large screened-in porch just off their bedroom. "These are for Isabel and Timothy," Roy explained. His half of the room was just on the other side of a cloth screen dividing the porch.

"But, Roy, the children will disturb your studies," Jean remonstrated, thinking of Isabel not quite five, and Timothy a lively three and a half.

"I'm sure I can handle them if they get obstreperous! I used to take care of my little sister, Elaine. I love children and would enjoy having them." To the family's surprise, this remained a happy arrangement throughout the year before Roy's wedding. The children grew to love "Uncle Roy," and he was a blessing to their very busy mother.

During this year there came persistent tales from Meo-land of a "Meo King" who was calling for the support of the whole tribe and promising *Utopia* in return. Even several whole villages set out to move back into China to follow this "King". As such activities increased, Roy wrote to his prayer partners: "Friends, I beg you to give earnest prayer for the Meo Christians and the two lady missionaries in Palm Leaf now. Gillian and I are due to join them after we are married, but at present the future of the work is in jeopardy. Trouble has begun in the hills and the 'Meo King' group has been told to get rid of all foreigners and non-supporters. This has resulted in someone trying to set fire to the ladies' house in Palm Leaf village while they were sleeping. To leave the village would be the easiest way out, but both feel they cannot just leave the three Christian families to face the consequences, for the threat is also to all Christians. One family has already turned back through fear. We believe the will of God is the safest place for any Christian wherever that may lead, and the ladies believe that to stay in the village is God's will at present."

Gillian spent Christmas, 1960, in Chiengrai and was able to meet the Thai friends and make wedding arrangements. Roy had long wanted to have a Chiengrai wedding, but was not sure of accommodation or the catering. On making a few enquiries, he had found that the local friends were as keen to have the wedding there as he. Mrs. Tong Dee, the headmaster's wife, was full of ideas. She offered to supervise all the catering in good Thai style, with a sprinkling of foreign customs so as to assure them it was still Roy and Gillian's wedding! Gillian approved it all, and every minute was filled with joyful planning.

Roy wrote after her visit: "Gillian left this morning after a lovely week-end, and a really wonderful Christmas. Of course, we had much to talk about! Where will we be stationed? When will we be going to the Meo? So much is still uncertain, but we can trust the future plans to the Lord and enjoy the present blessings. I find a measure of excitement in looking into the future with God."

In another letter to friends in New Zealand, in March, he recounted: "I watched a fascinating play on Thai history at the Christian school the other evening, and was reminded that the curtain was slowly falling, as it were, on the First Act of my life in Thailand. The curtain will rise on Act Two, when in a few days I seek residence in Meo-land. Soon begins the time of packing and preparing a home for my bride among the Meo people. The serious situation has eased considerably, and Gillian and I plan to move to Namkhet village some time after the big occasion on April 27 here! The future bride and groom seem to be floating on air at present!"

Roy was able to spend three weeks in Namkhet, but arrangements for building a house were not finalized, after all. Some of the Meo were talking of moving, which was typical of their migratory patterns. The Christians there were at a low ebb spiritually, and there was fear that scattering would weaken them still further.

Roy came back to Chiengrai very thin and tired; rejoicing in the opportunities which lay ahead, but concerned because he had been unable to arrange for a house for their residence. One quiet evening while he was sitting over some work, Jean Nightingale said to him: "Well, in a few days you'll be meeting your Mum and Dad at the Bangkok airport!"

"It's wonderful they can come to the wedding! It's hard to realize that I haven't seen them for nearly two years!" Then the excitement in his eyes faded. "But I can't help feeling a little queer with things so uncertain. I guess it's natural for a man to want to have a home for his bride. My brothers in New Zealand had lovely homes, with everything ready, for their brides; but all I have to offer Gill is some shack on a hillside that isn't even built yet, with no modern conveniences or anything! I'm quite looking forward to the rugged mountain life and primitive conditions, myself, but it's not what a man thinks of offering his wife."

"But, Roy," Jean protested, "remember that Gillian is a soldier of the Cross, too! I'm sure she is not expecting an easy way ahead. She's already spent two months with the ladies in Palm Leaf, learning how to cope with primitive housekeeping. I think she's just as ready and eager to start this life as you are."

"You're right, of course," Roy said, his face clearing. "When I visited her in Palm Leaf just recently, she was thrilled at the privilege of living in a Meo village and seemed to be enjoying it! She told me, 'The Lord's step from His throne in glory to the Cross leaves me no room to think that I've done anything to be proud of in coming from England to a Meo village.' What's a fellow got to complain about when he has a girl like Gill to face life together with him!"

The wedding-day dawned bright and fresh after a heavy

shower the night before. Thai Christian friends had decorated the church and prepared the school grounds for the reception. In the living-room of the Mission home many hands were busy arranging roses and *gerberas* in a profusion of shades. Roy had just come in with several sprays of spider-orchids which he had found in a tree in the front garden. He watched his mother as she arranged them with red roses in a dainty basket for his bride. At the other end of the table Jean was organizing a group to prepare food for the noon meal, while small Timothy clamoured for her attention.

"I'll take Timothy down the street with me," Roy offered.

"Not on your wedding-day!"

"Why not? I've got nothing else to do—the groom's just in the way at the moment! And Timothy's lost in this crowd." So Roy took time to buy a lively little boy a new toy jeep. No wonder the children loved him.

The first guests to arrive at the church that afternoon were the Chiengrai Governor and a group of Yao tribal Christians. Missionary guests from Australia, England, South Africa and America, and even some B.T.I. classmates from New Zealand, mingled with Christians of different tribes and peoples. It was a moving testimony to the unity there is in Christ Jesus. Then, the ceremony over, Roy and Gillian walked down the aisle together, thrilled at last to be man and wife.

"You are smiling too much," Mrs. Tong Dee cautioned quietly as they passed her, reminding them that in the eyes of the Thai it is not seemly to show one's feelings openly. Outside the church, Roy bent to whisper to Gillian, "You can't expect us not to smile after we've waited so long for this!"

The reception at the Christian school was a delightful combination of Eastern and Western customs. Mr. Tong Dee, master of ceremonies, was in his element. Mr. Orpin, Sr., had the joy of presenting a Bible to Roy and Gillian as a token of love from Roy's home church in New Zealand. This was followed by a curry and rice meal, accompanied by music from a Thai orchestra. Then, the meaning of the whole reception was brought to a climax by the duet, *Calvary*, sung by Roy and Gillian as their testimony.

So much more, O Saviour, show me
Of the meaning of Thy cross,
Break to me the bread of Calv'ry
Lest my soul should feed on dross.

So much more endue my spirit
With the fire of Thy love,
Break to me the bread of Calv'ry
Pour Thy Spirit from above.

So much more let faith be reckless,
Freed from all the world's decay;
Lay up treasure in the heavens
That survive the Judgment Day.

So much more let Christ victorious,
Who from sin has made us free,
Reign in life in earth, in Heaven,
And be praised eternally.

So much more may we united
Bear Thy Name to men oppressed,
Break to them the Bread of Calv'ry
Bless their souls as we are blessed.

The young couple spent the honeymoon in a lovely little Thai house on the mountain above Chiengmai; a cottage surrounded by pine trees and a rose garden; an ideal spot in every way.

"Gill," Roy said one day, "I wish we could stay on and live in this little house. It's our first home. There's that Meo village nearby and we could carry on Meo work even at our very doorstep! . . . But this would be the easy way out," he quickly admitted. And it was not the easy way the Master was leading these two.

They came down the mountain to Chiengmai feeling full of energy and ready to face the task He had set before them. One evening, after a long talk with the Heimbachs about the Meo and what their next step should be, Roy said to Gillian, "It seems to me we are facing the toughest time we've ever experienced both physically and spiritually."

"I feel the same way, Roy," Gillian answered. "I feel totally inadequate *myself*, but feel challenged to see what God will do for us as we enter this situation. The Lord is bound to have all the glory, as our utter weakness casts us completely upon Him!"

"That was a wonderful verse that was given us on our wedding-day," Roy reflected. "Colossians 1.11, Phillips' translation. 'As you live this new life, we pray that you will be strengthened from God's boundless resources, so that you will find yourselves able to pass through any experience and endure it with courage'. . . . *through any experience* . . . why that takes in everything, doesn't it?"

Roy left for Namkhet on May 24, this time to look for a house to buy as so many Meo were moving away. Many well-built houses were often abandoned to the fast-growing jungle. He returned after several days with exciting news: "Surprise! I've got a house!" he greeted Gillian triumphantly.

"Praise the Lord! Tell me about it!"

"Well, Norgo, one of the Christians, has promised us his house when he moves to Cawca, but that may not be for another two or three months. Then I found that one whole section of the village, quite distant from the Christians, has been vacated by people moving to Big Mountain. One man I talked to agreed to sell me his house for 30 *baht*. That's about ten shillings! Cheap, don't you think?"

"But at that price what condition is it in?" Gillian asked dubiously.

"It's not bad; it's been a well-built Meo house with a walled-off bedroom, and it even has two small tables and a rice pounder where we can mill our own rice! It was quite a mess at first, of course. The doors wouldn't shut properly. When I tried to prop them up, my friend the pig just pushed them down again. But then I saw his usefulness. There's plenty in a Meo house for a pig to eat, so I finally let him stay and eat all the old corn and general junk I scraped out of the corners. The house is in reasonably good order now. I left it shut up with a good lock on the front door. Mr. Pig can't get in now while I'm away."

On June 1, they were off to Meo-land at last! With a night's travel by train, they arrived at Pitsanuloke about three in the morning. The next day, somewhat bleary-eyed, they squeezed into a local bus for the journey along the wilderness highway to where the hill trail to the Meo began. About 10 a.m. they disembarked and while the bus continued on its way they sat down on their boxes and baskets at the side of the road.

"Ying was supposed to be here with the horses," Roy said gloomily as two hours went by with no sign of the Meo. Had he misunderstood? Would they have to spend the night in this lonely spot?

"I think I hear bells," Gill said suddenly. "I think they're coming!" They watched the trail and soon Ying, with two little boys and four horses, emerged from the jungle. Ying had a sheepish grin. He was sorry he was late, but it was too difficult to explain why with his poor grasp of spoken Thai.

There was little they could do to help in the loading. It is a fine Meo art to lift by hand and guess the weight without any instrument whatsoever. It takes infinite patience as each load in turn is reckoned for weight, and bits from one box are added to another to get just the right balance. This took three more hours as Ying had to do it all alone.

"Why didn't Simon come along? He sent his horse. Why did they leave it all to Ying?" Roy wondered impatiently. "I guess it's just their way and we had better try to get used to it." But the waiting was frustrating; without explanation, it appeared to be such a waste of time.

When they had gone an hour or more up the trail, Roy found out why Ying had taken so much time balancing the loads just right. Simon's horse was temperamental and something was uncomfortable. Rearing suddenly, he threw himself backwards and rolled over on his load, the tin boxes crunching and twisting ominously.

"Now I know why the boxes of Meo workers are so dented," laughed Gillian when she had recovered from her first startled dismay. Ying and Roy had disentangled the horse, unhurt, and to their wonder found nothing was damaged in the boxes. Ying hid a 28 lb. tin of milk powder in the damp jungle to bring up later, and distributed the rest of the load among the other horses. That was another hour gone.

They continued on, but since Simon's horse was slowing them up, Ying sent Roy and Gillian on ahead with the two Meo lads. Night fell before they reached Namkhet so that the last part of the journey was in dense darkness. Roy held the lead of one of the horses and Gill followed on blindly, both stumbling many times.

"Where are you, Roy?" Gillian called several times, and Roy answering would wait until she had picked herself out of the rocky creek bed and caught up. It was about 10 p.m. as, weary and bruised, they neared the shanty. Thoughts of how nice it would be to open the place and get a fire going had spurred them on. But the shanty stood squat and dark. Something was different; something was wrong!

"What's happened here?" Roy cried as he moved nearer. "The door's been broken down!" They stumbled in over debris and groped their way inside. Fumbling in his pack, Roy found two candles and lit them. Anger coursed through him as the flickering light revealed the shambles of what had been a little home. The bedroom walls had been chopped up for firewood; the tables he had scrubbed with such loving care must have suffered the same fate. Who could have done this to them? But even as the words formed in his mind, he knew the Lord's rebuke. Here was an opportunity to prove the grace of God as sufficient. Here was one of the experiences Colossians referred to!

"Praise the Lord we've arrived!" Gillian exclaimed. "We do have a roof over our heads, Roy." Roy's shoulders straightened. It was so much easier to take the disappointments with Gillian's buoyant spirit to steady him. Apparently Thai traders or Meo travellers had spent the night here thinking this was just an abandoned house. He guessed all his efforts hadn't shown after all!

Roy felt he should go back to help Ying, though he was reluctant to leave Gillian with the cockroaches and only two candles for light. When he arrived back about one in the morning, he couldn't believe the changed appearance of the room. Gillian had found a small lamp; had a cheerful fire going on the earthen floor in good Meo fashion, and a simple supper of baked beans and toast ready, their first real meal of the day and eaten in their new home!

"Pray that we will learn to be *glad* in disappointments that are only to our desires, glad to know the sufficiency of His grace," Roy asked later, writing to prayer partners of this experience. "Will you pledge yourselves anew to your task to stand fast with us, and let us watch that we really believe God will give what we ask for."

CHAPTER SIX

LAUGHS AND FRUSTRATIONS

"IT'S wonderful to be here at last!" Gillian said again as they sat next morning eating their meagre breakfast, their table an upturned pig trough! Much of the debris was still evident as they had been too weary to be thorough. "So different from all our plans for our first home together," she laughed, then added quickly, "But I really wouldn't have it otherwise. Maybe we are being tested to trust." After only a few hours' rest, even in such surroundings, Gillian's spirit had risen and she was ready—even eager—to face the day, their first in this place of God's appointment.

"You've got plenty of courage, Gill," Roy said admiringly. "How about lending me some?" he teased.

Familiar voices broke in on them from the doorway. "Hello, there! Do you let strangers in?" They turned to see their fellow-workers from Palm Leaf Village smiling at their surprise.

"Dorothy! Doris!" Roy and Gillian called together and scrambled up to receive them.

"Well, the Lord must have sent us just at the right time," Dorothy said, looking about her. "We had no idea that you were here. Yesterday we came over from Palm Leaf to visit the Christians, and to our surprise this morning they told us you had arrived."

"Yes, we stumbled in in the dark," Roy laughed, "and were greeted with this," waving his hand at the chopped-up wall and general debris. "I thought I had only to guard against my friend, the pig, getting in; I didn't reckon on itinerant traders, or the easy matter it is to get into a Meo shanty! But how are you two? Come and have some coffee!"

It was amazing what four could do as things took shape and order in the following days. Dorothy Jones and Doris White-lock, both nurses and experienced in Meo, dealt with the numerous people who came to ask for medicines and treatment. They also helped with the business of bartering for rice and fat from the Meo. This was not an easy matter, since there was no market. The rice was unhulled, so Roy had his first experience in using the rice pounder, and Gillian the borrowed winnowing tray. There seemed so many things to learn all at once, just to live in a Meo village!

Roy enjoyed working on the house. He explored the nearby abandoned shanties for material and came back with an assortment of "treasure"—tables and benches, lengths of boards for shelves, and even such a useful article as a chopping-block. With hammer and nails, things began to take on a look of home and comfort.

"Who would have believed it could look so nice!" Doris exclaimed when Roy had everything in place and Gillian had fixed plastic curtains for a touch of colour. "With dining alcove, shelves, benches and goodness-knows-what!"

"It's clean and comfortable now and it's our home, temporary one though it be," Gillian said with warm pride in Roy's work.

During the week they were there, Dorothy and Doris took Roy and Gillian to visit in each of the Christians' homes. Roy had met some of them before, of course, but there was a kind of ceremony in this—a new beginning, as they took up their life together with these people.

"I think we had better leave tomorrow," Dorothy said on Wednesday evening after the prayer meeting at Norgo's house. "We must stop off at Bitter Bamboo to make arrangements with Zay for his breaking off opium smoking. He said he couldn't break at Palm Leaf, since all the men there are back to regular smoking. The Christians here say he should come to Namkhet.

We'll see how Zay feels about it. You may see us again in the next few months!"

"Come any time!" Roy and Gillian called together as they watched the two move off towards Bitter Bamboo the next morning. Roy was interested in Zay's story. He had been an influential *shaman*, a leading figure among the spirit worshippers, a crafty tool of the devil given to lying and deception. It was through the bold witness of Nia Bow and his family, and the demonstration of practical Christianity when so many neighbours were sick, that Zay and his wife had turned to the Lord. Namkhet Christians had gone over to Bitter Bamboo to help him destroy his paraphernalia, among which was the *ndrew ning*, a spirit drum. This was used at funerals, and it was rumoured that anyone who touched it would die. When Ying and Simon had boldly picked it up and sent it crashing down a steep ravine and had not died on the spot, the people were visibly impressed and awed.

It was strangely quiet after Dorothy and Doris left. Roy and Gillian's house was so isolated from the Christians they rarely saw them. Their only contact was when they visited them in their homes, or met them at the meetings, which were usually held in Mblia Dua's home.

The quiet did not last long. Non-Christians were not slow about visiting. Soon Roy and Gillian found that life in a tribal village was very full, and never dull, with people in and out of the house all day long. Even though they were so far removed from the rest of the village, numerous families on the move to the Big Mountain area were continually using the empty houses next to them as stopping-off places. Life was varied and full of surprises, sometimes with unexpected difficulties, sometimes comical.

Many of the villagers who came for medicine brought vegetables or fruit in exchange, or sometimes a bit of cash. But meat was scarce. One day Roy decided one of their cocky little roosters must be eaten. While he was getting it ready for the pot, a village woman came up to ask if he would buy her pineapple. She used a word he had not heard before and, quick to catch new phrases, he dashed into the house to find its meaning in their small dictionary. In the moment he was inside, the pig came snuffling along, saw the rooster and promptly appropriated it! By the time Roy had caught him, the wing-tips had been chewed off and it was rather a mess, but into the pot it went!

Roy found life with Gillian full of fun and laughter, and just what he needed to offset the frustrations that came so unexpectedly in a Meo village. He had heard some talk of coming down to earth with a bump after the honeymoon, but for them their love became more wonderful every day. Each evening, when the last caller had gone, Gillian would get cups of hot Ovaltine and as they sipped it they would talk of the day's happenings. Sometimes it was to laugh together over the absurd or amusing things; sometimes it was to share the problems, burdens, frustrations, or the Lord's Word to them individually.

"Wasn't it funny when the chopping block caught the eye of that man today," Roy mused as he covered the fire with ashes one evening. "He just helped himself, laughed, and walked out with it! It was such an absurd little laugh, that I had to laugh, too. Anyway," he added, "it may have been his, after all!" Gillian's gay laughter joined Roy's deeper chuckles at the memory. But some of the problems they faced were more serious than seeing their useful articles walk out in the arms of embarrassed but determined Meo. There was the problem of their Quiet Time. They both got up early to have time for Bible study and prayer before visitors began to arrive. But no matter how early they were, hardly would Roy get the small paraffin lamp lighted, than someone would come banging on the door.

One morning it was a man with a sore foot. He wanted to have it treated before going to work in the fields for the day. The patient satisfied, they had just settled down to their reading when there was another knock on the door. This time it was Ying. Leah, his wife, had been sick all night with a fever. Could they come? Gillian gathered together her nursing kit and they went at once to help.

When they returned, a crowd of boys came in with them, and without a word helped themselves to the use of the rice pounder. Wasn't this pounder made by one of their own relatives? They needed to hull enough rice for their return trip to Big Mountain.

With the loud talking and laughter of the boys, accompanied by the *clomp, clomp* of the rice pounder, there was no further opportunity for quiet. Since it was raining steadily by this time, they could not retreat outside the shanty for peace.

The noise went on all through the day. Finally, towards evening, Roy exclaimed impatiently, "I wish I could throw that rice pounder out of the door!" And then, a little sheepishly, "But we'll need it for our own rice! Of course, I wouldn't have anyone keep away, but when there's hardly a break all day I long for peace and quiet!"

Morning after morning they got up early. Invariably, moments after the lamp was lighted, someone would either pry open the door or rattle it till Roy opened up. Then, as often as not, the visitor would just come in to sit and look at them.

"Something's got to be done about our prayer time and study," he said one morning, feeling rather desperate. "I don't like to keep people standing outside, but at such an hour in the morning it's either that or be robbed of any time with the Lord for the whole day."

"Even with the door locked, I feel so strange when there are eyes glued to the cracks in the wall," Gillian confessed. "It's so hard to pray while I'm being watched, but I guess these are some of the things we must learn to endure gladly for Christ's sake."

"But we must somehow find adequate time for Bible study and prayer. I feel such a very poor missionary."

"Yes, we seem to have nothing but interruptions," Gillian agreed sympathetically. "I suppose it's the same for others in this kind of life, but I feel as you do. I've prayed so little since being here, yet never have I felt the need to pray more."

But more was to come. The valuable lessons of this month in their first house in Meo-land, which Roy was finding difficult to learn at the time, were not finished. The most trying experience was with relatives of the former owner when they returned from Big Mountain for supplies. One crowd of people on the move had just left, and Roy and Gillian were sitting outside their shanty one evening enjoying the unusual peace and quiet. It was short-lived. A large group of Meo suddenly appeared on the trail and approached the shanty. Without a word to Roy, they walked right in the door of their home. Children began chopping horse-feed on the floor; baskets of live chickens were stacked just inside the front door. Several women calmly began to cook their supper over the small fire on the floor, and folk made themselves comfortable on every available seat. Two men even lay down to have a smoke of opium!

Roy and Gillian, hiding their astonishment and annoyance, got out their record player and began playing the Gospel Recordings records they had. What did one do in a situation like this, anyway? Their Meo was certainly not equal to the situation and the visitors spoke little Thai.

Roy listened as they talked, and gathered enough to know that these were relatives of the former owner of the house and that the owner himself was on the way. "They don't seem to know anything about our negotiations for the house," he said to Gillian. "All we can do is continue playing the records over and over again and just try to be sociable till the owner comes, I guess—and pray for patience and love," he added swiftly.

"What's that racket behind the house?" Gillian asked wonderingly. "I'll carry on with the records while you see what's happening."

Roy found an indignant old woman examining the stable which he had put to other uses than originally intended. She had been throwing out the firewood he had stacked neatly there, and now began to scatter his chopped-up sugar cane, to make room for her horse! Roy tried to remonstrate with her, but she seemed not to understand anything he said. At long last, one of the men came out and persuaded her to leave the stable alone and just tie her horse outside.

Roy returned to Gillian. "It's very hard not to be annoyed and even angry at an invasion like this. Our house is already non-private as it is. There seems to be nothing that is ours—time, property, privacy! And what does this do for the preaching of the Gospel? I'd do anything to have a home that was *ours* . . . or would I?" he asked slowly.

Next morning he said to Gillian, "After my frustrated, impatient outburst yesterday, the Lord had a word for me! I was reading in Isaiah 41.10 and it was as though He spoke directly to me and said: 'Fear not, for *I* am with you. *I* will strengthen you, *I* will help you. *I* will uphold you with my victorious right hand.'"

He wrote a little later to his Superintendent: "After several days of no privacy from early in the morning until late at night, I felt I couldn't stand much more. There seemed to be no secret place to go, for it had rained for days, and every space in the house had been invaded with 'visitors'. It seemed that only grace from above, given, not where weakness failed, but in the place of weakness, could bring me joy in the present situation. That is exactly what the Lord did for me, and now crowds don't worry me any more! That is, unless I want to try to write a letter to you and have to put up with a dozen grimy faces peering over my shoulders while they chew on ancient meat in my ear!"

Roy came dashing into the little house the last day in June and called out: "Gill, Norgo's moved! We can start shifting our stuff. I'm going down to look the place over, now. Want to come?"

It was a twenty-minute walk over to the main village, and when they got to the site Gillian exclaimed: "Oh, Roy! Isn't it lovely! I'm going to love this place! Look at that view—the jungle-covered hills stretching right down to the plains. We'll be able to watch lovely sunsets together from here!"

They strolled round the house, when Roy suddenly exclaimed in surprise, "Look! the pigs and chickens have burrowed under the bedroom walls so much that they're collapsing! I wonder why Norgo let the place deteriorate so much over the last weeks. He knew we were moving in. After all, we had paid him for his house."

"Well, I guess you can't expect too much when the two houses together only cost about £2," Gillian commented philosophically.

So their move began. All that twelve horses and six men had carried up the mountain, together with fourteen chickens, and the furniture Roy had made or mended, had to be moved over. Jahu, quiet and retiring, offered to help. As it turned out, he was the only one who did offer and he was the one with poorest health. It was back-breaking work negotiating the muddy trail, for there had been torrential rains. With a heavy pack on his back and carrying boxes or articles of furniture, Roy had difficulty keeping his footing on the steep, slippery places. Balancing on a tree-trunk over a dashing mountain stream held breath-taking possibilities, too. Sometimes, while manipulating a slippery spot with an extra heavy load, he would meet one or more of the Christians. "Oh, haven't you finished moving yet?" they invariably exclaimed.

He was deeply disappointed that no one else offered to help. He could not understand it. After all they *had* been invited here: to help teach those who understood Thai, and in turn be taught the Meo language. And yet none seemed to care enough to help. "By the time the move had been completed, which took five days, I had to ask special grace again from the Lord," he wrote to Ernie Heimbach at the time. "The verse the Lord gave me was Isaiah 49.5, 'My God shall become my strength'. I found the Meo, Christian and non-Christian, most exasperating, for as soon as they'd see me come over the hill with a load, they'd swarm down to the house. Then as soon as the door was opened they would rush in to see what they could pick up of Norgo's remaining things.

"Until I got a lock on the bedroom door, I'm afraid I had a full-time job taking things off people or trying to explain the best I could that Norgo had not moved completely and that nothing was to go. Several non-Christian women claimed Norgo had promised a certain piece of equipment that caught their eye. They were indignant when I refused permission to take it away. I found later that Norgo had made no such promises.

"Although God gave me grace to meet the need—Gill was scarcely concerned about the things that frustrated me—I found that gradually I was losing faith in the Christians. How much harder it is to bear the un-Christian conduct of Christians than the falsehoods of the heathen! A sense of mistrust of all Meo was taking hold of me."

The low spiritual condition of the church only added to this feeling. No sooner was the move complete than the Christians began to quarrel over who should get the leaf roofing from Roy's old house! "I had to be particularly careful," he wrote, "to be in the right mind when I went to speak to the offender, for I was not pleased about the covetousness of the people. Gill and I let it go for a few days and prayed about it. And when I went to see him, he understood and was agreeable to my suggestions."

A further matter for concern was the Sunday services held in Mblia Dua's home. Mblia Dua himself, because of his age, had influence among the others, but his testimony was being dulled now by his strong temptation to take a heathen wife. Simon, his eldest son, who with his family lived with Mblia Dua, was a young man with an attractive personality and a way of speaking that captured and held the attention even of unbelievers. But with his gifts, he lacked discipline in his study of the Word of God. He was unstable, sometimes rejoicing and inspiring others, sometimes moody and sullen, unwilling to take his part in leadership.

Nzoe, youngest son of Mblia Dua, was quite the opposite. Quiet and reserved, he loved to study. He had learned Thai and was now making his own translation of I John from the Thai Bible. He had recently married pretty little Choong, the grand-daughter of Mrs. Chieh Shaw. Her father, however, was an opium addict and though a professing Christian living over in Big Mountain, was making trouble for Nzoe concerning Choong's bridal price.

Leah, Mblia Dua's pampered youngest daughter and an immature Christian, had recently married Ying, the young man in his early twenties who had been threatened by his own unbelieving relatives for his bold Christian stand. Upon Ying had largely fallen the leadership of the church because he was the one who showed most spiritual life, but this leadership was not without its trials and discouragements.

One Sunday, Roy and Gillian went down to Mblia Dua's for the morning service. Folk were slow in gathering. First to arrive was Mrs. Chieh Shaw, a near neighbour of theirs. Sitting down on a low stool, she pulled out her glasses and tied them on with a bit of string. Opening her hymn-book, she began slowly to pick out the words of a favourite hymn. Although quite elderly, she had with firm determination and perseverance learned to read. Her husband had been the first Christian to die, and his death had been a triumphant testimony to all. Mrs. Chieh Shaw always prayed fervently for her absent sons: Choong's father had never showed any signs of spiritual life and had caused his mother many tears. Another son, Nia Bow, and his family, had moved to Bitter Bamboo where there was much hostility to the Gospel, but their quiet testimony there had broken down much prejudice, and several families had turned to the Lord.

Mrs. Chieh Shaw was soon joined by her son, Jahu, and his family who still lived with her. Though often weak and sickly, he was full of love for the Lord, ever since his deliverance from opium smoking and planting. Finally, with the arrival of several others, came Mrs. Ba Chu who, in spite of violent opposition from her unbelieving family, faithfully attended every service.

The meeting began, but Mblia Dua's family continued working: one chopping food for the horse and another feeding the pigs, while the children ran in and out noisily. It was difficult to get started amid such confusion and disorder.

After the usual hymn singing, led by Simon, Nzoe began to speak. At the church meeting the year before, called because of the threats against the believers by the "Meo King" group, it was Nzoe who had said quietly but firmly, "If we die, we die for the Lord Jesus." Yet now, reading from his translation of I John he sat with his back to everyone and spoke into his book! Was it because of shyness? He is probably giving a good word, Roy thought, but if no one can hear him what is the use of it?

Then Ying got up. "You children sit down and keep quiet!" he ordered. "We are in God's presence and no one is to talk." He spoke with authority, and immediately all chatting ceased. His was a well-prepared message and Roy felt this was the one encouraging portion of the whole service.

Each week-day evening Roy turned on the Thai Gospel broadcast, and a group of those who understood enough Thai gathered to listen. Often some stayed for a lesson in reading and writing Meo or Thai. One evening after all the others had gone, Ying stayed on for a talk. It finally came out that someone had sinned. He mentioned no names, but went on to tell how the result had been a chain reaction of anger and all sinning. He was burdened about the matter and had stayed to ask them to pray.

So the three of them knelt there in the small Meo shanty to pray for the Lord's stumbling children—with their testings and trials, their weaknesses and needs—and it was a very precious time together before the Lord.

After Ying had gone, Roy stirred up the fire while Gillian made the usual cup of Ovaltine. As they sat looking into the fire, Roy said: "I think what's behind all this is the problem of the bridal price. Nzoe and Ying have married daughters of professing Christian families, and there is ill-feeling between them as to whether a Christian should pay a bridal price or not. Simon has been quite worked up over it, I know. It seems, too, that Ying has married a problem child. He told me the other day that Leah wants to be like her mother, when she was living, and rule the home. 'But the Bible says that the husband is the head of the house,' Ying said firmly. 'And I intend to keep it that way.' I'm sure the problem isn't really that bad, but Ying is so sensitive, and is afraid of his testimony if his wife does not obey."

"It *is* strange that every time Ying wants to make a trip to Bitter Bamboo to teach the young Christians over there, Leah gets sick," Gillian mused. "The other day he returned soon after he had started out, saying that Leah didn't want him to go."

"Well . . . that did seem to be the Lord, anyway." Roy reminded her. "I persuaded Simon to go with Mrs. Chieh Shaw, and it turned out that Simon's brother-in-law wanted to burn his demon things that day and turn to the Lord. Simon was the very one they were looking for. He does seem to have the gifts of an evangelist. Then Mrs. Chieh Shaw was a great help where there was heated arguing. She is a dear soul, and seems always to know the right thing to say.

"These folk in Bitter Bamboo who have just burned their demon things are going to need a lot of help and teaching," Roy went on, returning to the important issue. "I hope Simon realizes this and doesn't leave it all to Ying. Their turning is only the initial step; it does not signify his brother-in-law has been born-again yet. It's teaching from the Word that the Spirit uses to give them life.

"This morning I had a wonderful time reading the Word, especially Colossians 1.28,29, where Paul speaks of his ministry to the Gentiles. He proclaimed, warned and *taught* every man that they would be presented mature in Christ. This was made possible by the energy which God mightily inspired in him. I feel this is our need here among the Meo church, and we need a gift of power to meet it, far beyond anything we have ever known before."

"Roy," Gillian said impulsively, "we've not been out of the village for some time. Let's visit Doe and Doris tomorrow! I think it would help us all to talk all these things over and pray together, don't you?"

"A good idea! But Palm Leaf's a ten-hour trek, remember. We'll have to get started early!"

CHAPTER SEVEN

A DESPERATE SITUATION

"IT was good to have that time in Palm Leaf," Roy said to Gillian some days later as they set out from their house to visit a patient in the village. "I hope Doe and Doris can get on with breaking Zay of the opium habit soon." After their visit to Palm Leaf, when the four White Meo missionaries had been able to discuss the perplexing problems of the work, they had all trekked back together as far as Bitter Bamboo. Leaving their two friends there, Roy and Gillian had returned to Namkhet, but had been thinking much of Zay and his battle with opium.

"It's a good thing we went when we did," Gillian commented. "Doe and Doris needed a man's help. I'm so glad you could put in those windows in their roof, fix the locks, and all. . . ."

"Yes, the Super ought to be pleased, too," Roy laughed, "since they presented me with most of the jobs they'd been saving for him! Well . . . speaking of angels! Look who's coming over the hill!" he shouted. Dorothy and Doris, accompanied by Zay from Bitter Bamboo, had just come into view through the trees.

"Zay has decided to do his opium breaking here in Namkhet," Doris explained as they met on the trail. "So we might be staying here a few weeks."

"It's a good thing I got the spare bedroom finished!" Roy teased.

"Any news about those two other families who burned their demon things the other day in Bitter Bamboo?" Gillian asked as they turned back to their house.

"Yes, we saw them yesterday. That makes three new families there now. They've turned from the demons all right, but they hardly know what it is all about as yet. They need teaching, urgently. Right now lots of people are scared stiff of the demons, all rushing to the demon priest. There is so much sickness and everyone seems terrified that something awful is going to happen. These new believers are going to be tested as never before, especially as some of the older believers are not giving a very good testimony."

Roy knew that one of these was Nia Bow and his family and he was not too surprised next morning when he heard Mrs. Chieh Shaw weeping bitterly. He went in to find her with Gillian and the other two around the log fire. Dorothy and Doris had confirmed a report that Nia Bow, whose Christian testimony had been a strong one in Bitter Bamboo, had now decided to plant opium again.

Mrs. Chieh Shaw's weeping for her son soon turned to fervent prayer, and then to decision. "I'm going right over there to talk to him!" she announced as she jumped up and left to begin preparations. Roy was deeply touched. He felt he should go with her, even though his feet were still sore from the Palm Leaf trek on which he had lost a toe-nail. But he found Mrs. Chieh Shaw had not waited for anyone, after all. In the afternoon, Roy and Ying talked and prayed together about the matter and early the next morning they set out for Bitter Bamboo.

"We arrived to find that Nia Bow was off doing his opium field and had no intention of returning right away," Roy recounted to the girls after he had returned to Namkhet, "so Mrs. Chieh Shaw had turned her attentions to the new believers and was having a little meeting in Soh's home. It did my heart good to hear her sing to the children, *in perfect tune*. It's only when others begin singing that she goes all haywire! Ying preached a nice 45-minute sermon to Soh who was extremely interested and full of questions. He said, 'We've torn out the demons, but really don't quite know what to do now.' Soh seems to be a very promising young man, full of go and questions, and seems genuinely to believe. He wanted to have a poster to explain to others. He's one of the few there who doesn't smoke opium. If his home is any indication of his industry he seems to be a bright fellow. We must pray that he will not be turned back by Nia Bow's sin, and that the Lord will really open his mind to the things of God. There were rumours that the relatives were going to gang up on him and the others." He turned to Dorothy, "How's Zay coming on in opium breaking?"

"He's been lying about how much he smokes," Dorothy said sadly. "He didn't have any craving yesterday, and I suspected that he'd been smoking. Today I found him in the act. He seemed sorry enough, and wanted to carry on. We didn't know what to do, but decided we should continue the course, as the Lord's honour is at stake."

"Sometimes it seems impossible that these people should be delivered from their bondage to demons and opium," Roy said, "but the Lord has been reminding me of a verse He gave me while I was in Singapore. Isa. 49.24-25: 'Shall the prey be taken from the mighty, or the lawful captive delivered? But thus saith the Lord, Even the captives of the mighty shall be taken away, and the prey of the terrible shall be delivered.' We must hold on in faith. . . .

"Here in Namkhet," he continued, "we need to pray for revival. The Lord's table has been neglected for two months now, and I feel we are giving Satan a wide-open door to enter if we let the church continue on this way. . . . And there's the meeting in Mblia Dua's home. Something *has* to be done about it. There's increasing lack of reverence every Lord's Day. . . ."

He broke off as Ying's voice was heard from the doorway. Roy called to him to come in, and to their surprise Ying went immediately to the point of his coming: his concern over the disorderly services of late and a request that they be allowed to meet again in the missionary's house. Roy was startled at this timing, and yet he hesitated. On the surface, it seemed a step backward from the indigenous policy. But as they talked it over it seemed the Lord had directed, and they agreed to allow it and to ask the Lord's help in teaching more of what it means to meet in worship.

At the following Sunday service Ying put the matter of the Lord's table before the whole group. His sincerity was moving and the weight of his burden was in the tones of grief in his voice as he said: "God will cast you off like He did Israel, if you continue to go on sinning and not desiring to meet with God." A subdued discussion followed and it was decided to hold a communion service that afternoon. No one was to come unless he had prepared his heart before the Lord.

That afternoon, Roy watched the baptized believers begin to gather. Nzoe was among them. It had been rumoured that Nzoe had consented to help his father-in-law make opium fields to gain the hand of Choong. Roy was glad Dorothy was here to deal with this problem. She put the question of opium quite frankly to Nzoe. He did not deny it; he was aware of his sin, and Roy's heart burned for him as, without a word, he rose and went out. A realization of the curse of sin in the lives of those who profess the Lord's Name swept over the small group gathered there to partake of the symbols of remembrance of His death, and sobered them.

After the meeting, a rota was drawn up for speakers to go across to Bitter Bamboo to lead meetings there, and also one for responsibility for leading and preaching at the Sunday services in Namkhet. Simon demurred when his name was put down. "I have no power," he said. "I can't take my share of preaching." Roy sensed a lack in Simon's life, but did not know how to deal with it and his heart was heavy with the knowledge that there was still so much here that was not right before God.

The climax came next morning when he heard of Zay's complete failure to break off opium. Roy pushed aside the breakfast dishes and leaned wearily against the wall behind his bench as Dorothy reviewed the failure in detail.

"Last night Zay threw off Jahu and the others who were caring for him. He ran out of the door to another house where he got the opium he was craving. Jahu told me this morning, 'He doesn't really have the heart to break with it.' "

"It's not surprising after the week of lying almost every day, and his immoral conduct the other night," Roy said heavily.

"I wonder at the wisdom of trying medically to help anyone to break with opium," Dorothy said thoughtfully. "All such have turned back, and those who broke by themselves because they loved the Lord and saw opium as sin, like Jahu, Mrs. Ba Chu, and Mblia Dua have stayed off it."

There was silence for a while as each of the missionaries thought of the past weeks with their brief encouragements so quickly overshadowed by disappointment and failure.

"There's been a whole series of defeats in the lives of Meo believers recently," Doris said quietly. "The three men in Palm Leaf have gone back to regular opium smoking. They get thinner every day, and one was even accused of *stealing* opium, so that the heathen are saying, 'The Christians aren't any different from the rest.' "

"Then there's Nia Bow's family in Bitter Bamboo," Dorothy went on. "I could have wept when talking to Mrs. Nia Bow the other day. They are far away from the Lord. It was heartbreaking. We could have no fellowship at all. I asked her how it all happened, and she said it began when her heathen parents came to live in the home, and brought opium with them. Nia Bow handled the stuff, preparing it for her father to smoke. 'We all feel we must plant it for we really need the money,' she added. Their hearts seem so unready to take any word of exhortation or rebuke or imploring that I wondered if I should say anything. Yet, as missionaries here, we have a responsibility to the Lord, however hard or heart-breaking it may be to carry out."

"There's all the sin in the Namkhet church, too," Gillian put in. "But I feel the Lord is warning many for getting away from Him. Mblia Dua's field-house burned down the other night and they lost their blankets and clothes. Then all of Nzoe's pigs died suddenly, when other people's pigs have remained quite well. I think they feel the Lord is speaking to them."

"With all this unconfessed sin, no wonder there's no blessing," Roy said. "I could weep sometimes at the hardness of heart.

Let's go out to the baptismal pool for prayer," he suggested. "It's a desperate situation, and we need to get alone where we can have undisturbed waiting on God."

Down the trail a short distance, Roy led the way through deep undergrowth and along to a stream which collected in a dark, green pool. They seated themselves on the rocks and Roy watched the water as it left the pool and dipped over the edge of the precipice to fall to the rocks far below. He felt that the matted jungle closed them off from the rest of the world, and in the quiet he could hear the unvoiced questions felt in each heart. Why darkness when there should be light? Why failure when there should be victory?

"I've been reading Zechariah four," Roy broke the silence, "and verses six and ten have come to me with real force. 'Not by might, nor by power, but by my spirit, saith the Lord of hosts.' I believe *a price must be paid*," he said slowly, "before the promise of verse ten, 'They shall rejoice', can mean anything to us. Ever since our arrival in Namkhet, we have been fighting against a solid wall of resistance. We seem to be powerless in prayer and the Spirit just doesn't seem to be at work among us."

"If we really want revival in the Meo church," Dorothy agreed, "we must be prepared *to pay any cost*." Again there was silence as each searched his own heart as to what that cost might mean.

"I've been challenged by some thoughts of Mr. Sanders'," Doris said, "so much so that I made some notes in my Bible. Maybe you've read this before, but listen: 'Mastering the art of praying in the Spirit will take time. . . . We each have all the time there is and we each choose our own priorities. We automatically place first that which we deem most important. If prayer is meagre, it is because we consider it supplemental, not fundamental. To our Lord it was not a reluctant addendum, but a fundamental necessity. . . . Prayer is spiritual warfare. . . . We see souls bound in sin, but our concern in prayer should be not only to pray *for them*, but also to pray *against Satan* who holds them captive. . . . The advance we long to see on every field will come only as the adversary is deposed, and that can be done only by aggressive praying.'

"Don't you think," she added slowly, "that more would be accomplished if all the Meo team of workers met for a time of prayer and fasting, instead of wasting time up here as we seem to be doing at present? This place is like the valley of dry bones, and we need the breath of God upon us. . . . Beginning with me."

The suggestion met instant response in each burdened heart and after prayer together, they agreed to write to the Superintendent and suggest the Meo team meet together in Chiengmai for a time of prayer and fasting for the whole of the Meo field. Doris wrote for the group: "We are suggesting that all the Meo team of workers come up to Chiengmai for a season of discussion, prayer and fasting, as the Spirit leads. Don't think we're defeated by all the heartaches and failure. We're not! We're full of praise that He is not only showing us our need, but showing us how that need can be met in Himself. When He, the Holy Spirit, comes upon us, as we believe He will, then there's going to be a song of rejoicing redounding to His glory through these hills."

Little did Roy realize where that victory would begin, and scarcely did he think that it must begin with him, and with each one of the Meo team.

"I feel I hardly know how to spend an *hour* in prayer, not to speak of praying for a week or more," Gillian confessed as they set out one morning near the agreed time, to descend to the plain from their mountain village. They had had heavy rain for weeks, but this had not daunted them. The trail was deep with mud and they slithered down red clay slopes and across soggy gorges. Gillian had just stopped to scrape the mud from her shoes in a little stream they were crossing.

"If this is of the Lord, as we believe it is," Roy assured her, "I'm confident the Holy Spirit will pour out upon us a spirit of prayer. We won't have to *try* to pray."

Just then a rumbling in the distant jungle caught their attention. The roaring increased like the fast approach of a train, and before they could move very far a tropical cloud-burst was upon them, soaking them. It seemed a long way still to the hotel at Pitsanuloke and a change of clothes. But they reached the town at last, and a comfortable train journey brought them eventually to Chiengmai—the last of the team to gather.

It was exciting to see the whole Meo team, and especially Don and Kathy Rulison who had just returned from furlough. Roy felt a oneness of purpose knitting his heart to the other nine members of the team. All felt as desperate about the situation as he did, and were determined to seek the Lord unitedly.

There were no planned meetings, but the Lord led each day in private and united times of prayer. Sometimes sessions lasted over five hours, but none of the team was conscious of the time. Prayer was intense, and fasting easy. Although there were no assigned messages it was obvious to Roy that the Lord had done some serious speaking to all concerned. It was a tremendous encouragement to him to hear one and another share what was on his heart. He, himself, spoke of the Lord's message to him from Zechariah four, and in turn was challenged as an article about Jonathan Edwards was read: who during days of prayer and fasting had cried, "God give me New England!"

"God give us the Meo," Roy prayed. Questions piled into his mind and stirred his heart. "What do we mean by 'God give us the Meo'? What do we really expect? Three men in Palm Leaf delivered from opium? A few families saved? Children coming to learn to read? Is this all? Is this the radical work of the Spirit we expect? *Are we asking for a little thing? Or a big thing?*"

" 'Thus saith the Lord God; I will yet for this be enquired of by the house of Israel . . .' (by the Meo team)," one began to read, and Roy's heart leapt in response, " 'to do it for them; I will increase them with men like a flock': Ezekiel 36.37. Here is a promise God has given, but are we willing to pay the price to see it fulfilled? He is waiting for us to ask! *Have we been watering down the promises of God? Do we really believe He will do all that He has promised?*"

On Saturday, reports were given from each station. It was a sombre picture: no new converts from among the Blue Meo for several years; two of the new believers in Bitter Bamboo gone back to the demons after only two weeks' profession, Soh being one of them; most of the Christians lacking in evangelistic zeal;

sparse evidence of spiritual leadership emerging; no burden or
vision for the salvation of their own people; the heathen Meo
in their thousands virtually unreached.

The burden of prayer lay heavily upon Roy and his team-
mates. The keen desire for the Lord to work in Meo hearts
pressed them to their knees. But God had a deeper work to do in
their hearts. There was to be a costly cleansing of things of
which they were as yet unconscious.

Roy had never felt as desperate as he did that night. He could
not sleep, and the session that day with his report on Namkhet
kept running through his mind. The Meo Christians *wanted*
victory over sin. Mblia Dua quarrelled in his home, but he did
not really want to. Mrs. Chieh Shaw felt no power in prayer,
though she prayed fervently for her wayward sons. At the last
Lord's table, just before he and Gillian had come down from the
mountain, all had wept because they felt so far from the Lord.
They *were* hungry for better things. How could he help them
when he felt so powerless himself? He had prayed for days now,
and yet he longed for a special word of assurance of how God
was going to meet his need. How could he go back to the village
unless he had a fresh word from the Lord for himself personally?
There was the solid wall of resistance among the heathen. Clan
solidarity had forced the new believers back. They could not
stand when the relatives put the pressure on. There was the
awful hold opium had upon Christians and non-Christians alike.
The deep, underlying fear of demons gripped hearts. All this
combined to make a mighty barrier against the knowledge of
God.

The curtains at the window stirred, and a cool breeze brought
welcome relief from the humid night. A few drops of rain
sprinkled on his face. He pulled the sheet tighter around him. It
was nice to be in a house not smoked up by a log fire. He
thought of going back to the lack of privacy, the thoughtlessness
of the Christians, the grime, the filth, the toil, the mud, and
the lies. Suddenly, he became aware of the wall in his own
heart. *He saw the barrier between him and the Meo was his own
coldness of heart.* He lay stricken before the revelation of his lack
of genuine love, his selfish hold on things, his unwillingness

to spend and be spent. "Oh, God, forgive me," he cried in his spirit.

Early dawn was breaking and the birds in the spreading mango tree began their welcome to a new day. Roy sat up and looked out of the window. Blossoms from the jacaranda tree made a carpet of lavender on the green lawn. His heart responded to the beauty around him. "Be still and know that I am God," he whispered. He opened his Bible to Psalm 46 and began to read: "God is our refuge and strength . . . God is in the midst of her . . . God shall help her, and that right early." The words came alive. Never before had Scripture seemed so plain to him. This was God's answer to his heart's cry for a fresh word from Him, and promise for Namkhet. Now he could go back to the village! Joy and love flooded his heart that the Lord should want him back after all his failures. God was with him, and this fresh realization made all the difference. Truly, a new day had dawned for Roy.

He found that God had been dealing with others through the night, and at the united meeting he shared his recent experience. "I have known times of heart-searching before," he said, "but never has it been revealed to me that *my cold heart was actually withholding blessing, and even salvation, from others* . . . I feel now that I can go back to the spiritual battle in Namkhet. I have never been in a real battle before going up to live with the Meo, but I realize now that the battle is not mine but God's. II Chronicles 20.17 is also God's answer to me for returning to the Meo: 'Ye shall not need to fight in this battle: set yourselves'—in prayer, I believe He means for me—'stand . . . still, and see the salvation of the Lord with you . . . go . . . for the Lord will be with you.' If God has so worked in our little team of missionaries, surely He will do the same among the Meo. He *will* cleanse His church, and revive their evangelistic zeal."

"Should we not join together in a covenant," the Super-intendent suggested, "to pray that the Lord will grant revival throughout our whole field? We get what we ask for when we determine at any price to have it; not for our glory, but His, Continual persevering prayer is essential if we are to see the spiritual quickening God has promised us."

Roy recorded in his notebook the prayer covenant that was then drawn up:

1. For the revival of the Meo church, with the conviction that it has already begun.
2. For a great turning to Christ among the heathen apart from *when*, *how*, or *where* it will begin.
3. For a spiritual quickening in every tribe and people throughout the whole North Thailand field, and the whole of the Mission.

The burden was now lifted, and the final period of prayer ended with a precious time around the Lord's table. Roy sensed there was a new lowliness before the Cross, but with it an overwhelming joy. He felt a closeness that bound his heart to each of the others, for he found the nearer to the Cross he came, the nearer he was to his team-mates. "Oh, may the blessings received here," he prayed, "be just a beginning of richer things in store for the whole Mission family."

CHAPTER EIGHT

CHANGE AND CHALLENGE

THE trail was as bad as ever as Roy and Gillian began the climb back up to Namkhet, but there was a spring in their steps. "I'm so anxious to get back and see what the Lord is going to do for us," Gillian said eagerly.

"I little thought that the tragedy of Zay's failure would become the beginning of better things," Roy said. "I feel now that we have a new faith to see greater things, and a willingness to pay any cost to see God's promises fulfilled."

The village scene was a different one for Roy, now. The Christians crowded around in warm welcome as he opened up their house again. Everything was intact, though rather mouldy for being left nearly two weeks. One of the Christians hurried in with live coals from his house and soon the fire was burning cheerfully. Roy found his heart moved and warmed with the welcome they had received. But it was not only that. It really was a joy to be back among the people again. God had put a new love in his heart for them.

The following days were busy and full of interruptions. Nothing had changed in that respect, but with a new attitude the interruptions failed to vex Roy as they once had done. He was here to serve.

One day, one of Mrs. Chieh Shaw's sisters came to ask them to help her son who had been taken very ill in the fields. It was a four-hour hike, but Gillian and Roy set out immediately. They found the young man extremely ill, but Gillian was able to see him responding to the medicines she could give before they set out on their return trip. As they neared the village, they were suddenly arrested by the familiar sound of the drum used to drive the demons away, the thin wail of the bamboo flutes, and the shrieks and moans of the women mourners at a death-wake.

"Who's died, I wonder?" Roy murmured as they pressed on into the village.

"It is Mrs. Ba Chu's husband," they were told. "Mrs. Ba Chu has moved in with a neighbour as her son insists on doing demon worship for his father's departed spirit."

Roy and Gillian hurried on to find Mrs. Ba Chu to give what comfort they could. They learned that her husband had been taken ill in the village by the road and his relatives had carried him home, where he had died in a few hours. She rocked back and forth in her grief as she told them. "He died without the Lord," she wept. "He would never listen to me when I tried to tell him. Only a few days ago he said, 'I don't want your Saviour.' And now he is dead, and my son insists on doing demon worship for his spirit. Oh, do pray for my son and his family," she cried.

Roy could get little satisfaction when he approached the son. He seemed more opposed than ever, and was insistent on the full rites for his father. While he was there, Roy turned to the crowd who had come to watch, and began to witness to them, surprised and thrilled that he was unafraid and that in spite of his still

E

limited Meo he had freedom in speaking. "I don't know whether it was imagination or not, but they seemed far more ready to listen," he reported back to Gillian.

But the noise of the demon rites reached to every part of the village until it was difficult to concentrate on prayer or work. "Let's go out to the baptismal pool for the day," Roy suggested one morning. Collecting Bibles and hymn-books and pieces of plastic sheeting for protection from the rain, they set out for the lovely little pool. Roy chose the spot by the edge of the waterfall where with Dorothy and Doris they had met that memorable day to pray. When it began to rain, he said determinedly, "We're not going home." Soon he had rigged up a shelter out of bamboo, banana leaves, and plastic sheeting. It kept them quite dry and they were able to have a long, undisturbed time of intercession for their people.

This Day of Prayer became a regular part of their lives. Every Tuesday, whether wet or dry, Roy shut up the house and he and Gillian went off for the whole day. He had made a more permanent shelter there, and though it rained most of the time, they were quite cosy. The villagers accepted the fact that they were never home on Tuesdays. Minds and spirits were kept fresh by this regular day alone with God, and they were learning how to battle against the powers of darkness that held the Meo in bondage. There they could unburden their hearts in prayer and tears for the deliverance of the people. This kind of praying cost, for it involved fasting, discipline, and persistency, but there was a joy and refreshing in it, too.

"I believe the Lord is teaching me to see Himself being formed in the believers, instead of their multitude of little sins," Roy confessed on one of their days of prayer. "Look at Ying. What a help he's been to me! With his help in teaching, I've been able to preach two messages in Meo. And the people really seem to take it in.

"And there's the restored fellowship round the Lord's table," he continued. When Roy had explained *why* they had gone to Chiengmai, several of the Christians had been much moved and had poured out their hearts to God in prayer for a similar work in their own hearts and lives. Some had begun to come in the mornings early to pray with Roy and Gillian for the lost Meo in their mountains.

"There certainly is a healthier and happier atmosphere in Namkhet," Roy concluded.

"It was fun putting on that big meal for the Christians," Gillian said. "I feel so much closer to them now!" They had been able to buy two large fish from some of the villagers and Gillian and Roy had invited the believers, following the Lord's Supper, to come and partake with them. Halfway through the meal a family had come in who had not been to a meeting for weeks. They had known nothing of the invitation to the meal. "It seems to have done them good," Roy remarked now, "and they realize they miss out in fellowship when they aren't regular. Have you noticed that they've been to every meeting since then?"

They laughed together, and Roy went on recounting blessings. "I'm specially happy about Jahu's eagerness to read. He wants to be able to take his place leading in services. And Ying is coming along for regular Bible study, too."

"But it would be false to say everything is all right," cautioned Gillian.

"No, we still have problems, but the Lord is gradually bringing about His victory in the lives of His people," Roy answered. "This strange 'flu that's hit only the Christians, I feel, is of the Lord. He had to bring Ying even to the point where he thought he was dying, before he and Leah both realized they needed each other."

Ying's family had been extremely antagonistic to the Gospel when he believed, and had persecuted him not a little for his faith. Then Drew, his younger brother, had come to visit Ying, bringing his wife, and said that he wanted to become a Christian and live with them. He began to attend Bible study classes and showed much promise. But one day Ying came to Roy, broken-hearted because Leah had told him both Drew and his wife must leave the house because she wanted it to herself. She had refused to talk or eat with any of them after that.

"What shall I do?" Ying had cried. "If Drew goes back to my father's house, he will most certainly return to the demon way.

And now my mother has also said she wants to come and live with us and maybe become a Christian, for she feels she couldn't do so, living at home. But Leah says *No*."

And then both Ying and Leah took suddenly ill with the 'flu. In Ying's case it turned to pneumonia and Gillian went several times to give him penicillin. He thought he was dying, and later told Roy that he had dreamed he got to Heaven but the Lord had sent him back again! Slowly, he recovered and Leah had begun to relent. She had not put things wholly right with God yet, but the situation in the home had improved.

"So many have needed special medical care, and it is right here that I feel we've learned to share things that before we have refused," Roy went on with his recounting. "The Lord has helped us let go our hold on things. By this we can show them we mean what we say when we tell about Christ's love."

"It seems like a big load lifted from my heart," Gillian confessed. "It's good to feel free to share milk and anything we have to strengthen those weakened by 'flu."

"Yes, before I wouldn't share what I'd carried up on my back. They could carry their own supplies! But I don't feel that way now. It's all joy, when it's given as medicine with a double dose of love!" Even the quagmire outside the back door that had been transformed into a nice garden, was contributing its share of tasty beans for their sick patients.

It was not surprising that during this same period the Enemy was making his counter-attacks. There were a number of means by which he endeavoured to discourage Roy and make him doubt that God would work according to the vision given during the days in Chiengmai. In September, soon after Roy and Gillian's return, there began a series of murders and robberies such as had never been experienced in the Meo work. The first of these occurred right in Namkhet. One night Roy was suddenly awakened by the sound of gunshot reports nearby.

"What's that?" Gillian asked nervously.

"I don't know. Strange for someone to be testing his gun at this time of night. But you can't put it past a Meo if his spirit moves him to fix his gun in the middle of the night!"

The next morning Roy was shooing the chickens out of the

house when a woman stopped by for medicine for her baby. "Did you hear what happened last night?" she asked as she swung the baby off her back and began to nurse it.

"No, what happened?"

"That Blue Meo man living just two houses down was murdered!"

A few days later, Thai police arrived. Roy and Gillian invited them to stay in their house while they were there, and Roy fixed up a big bed-platform for them in the living-room. One of the men was a Christian from Lomsak and he and Roy had a good time witnessing to the others before they went to bed.

In October, Roy heard rumours that Dorothy and Doris had been robbed and had lost most of their things. But as communications between Palm Leaf and Namkhet were poor at that season, it was several weeks before they had definite word. Then a note came across by a lad visiting his relatives. It was while they were all in Chiengmai that thieves had broken into the missionaries' house and stolen most of their things, including radio, gramophone, pressure lamp, and blankets. But Dorothy wrote joyfully of the Lord's goodness. "How big the little things seem at such a time. Things like clothes we had left here, which the thieves missed, so that we have a change; one blanket left and the loan of another from a Christian. And there are the big things, too, which are very precious to us—the Lord's giving of wonderful peace and joy. We haven't had to force ourselves to be cheerful. Then, on Sunday there was a closeness with the Christians which drew us all together in worship, and there's the confident assurance that while men have done this to us for evil, the Lord means it for good."

Roy's note back by the same lad mentioned plans to visit Palm Leaf soon to see how they could help. He added, "I've made a strong cupboard, with good locks, to store things in our bedroom, and I would suggest that if you can get some boards, I'll come across and make one for you, too. It may at least discourage petty thieves."

But before they could get away to Palm Leaf, they were surprised one afternoon to hear Ernie Heimbach's voice at the door. "Where did you come from?" Roy asked in astonishment.

"We thought you were on your way to Singapore for Overseas Council meetings."

"I am!" Ernie laughed. "But I thought I'd swing up here to visit you on my way out, to see how you were getting on. I've heard from Doris and Dorothy, but hadn't heard from you. I wondered if you were facing any of the Enemy's counter-attacks."

"We're all right," Roy said quickly. "Gill's just finished baking a pumpkin pie, in fact. Didn't know it was to welcome you!"

Ernie had come just at the right time. The Christians' hearts were hungry and ready for the working of the Holy Spirit. With his knowledge of Meo, Ernie came as God's messenger for the occasion. The people were excited to welcome him, and the next evening a large group gathered for a special meeting, when Ernie spoke on Achan. Hearts were stirred and a spirit of conviction was manifestly working as many sat with their heads bowed in their hands. Then Ying stood up, confessing his sins, and asked the forgiveness of those present. Others followed in confession. It was a solemn time and at the close a spirit of prayer took hold of them, and Mblia Dua prayed so humbly it moved Roy more than anything else. Yet he felt the work was not finished, and was much in prayer with Gillian and Ernie for the Sunday service next morning.

Nearly everyone was there. This time Ernie spoke on *Looking back and looking ahead*, using the story of Lot's wife who looked back, and Paul who forgot the things which are behind and pressed forward. Again, the Spirit of the Lord came upon them in conviction and confession. It was a tremendous joy to Roy and Gillian to hear Leah open her heart and confess her sins, and express her sincere desire to let the Lord give her a new heart.

Roy was moved to wonder to see these simple mountain people responding to the Word and to the voice of the Spirit by confessing their sins before the Lord and the whole church. He knew it was not according to custom for them to confess openly in this way. Yet some ended their confessions with: "If anyone here knows of other sins or faults I have committed, please tell me, and don't have regard for my 'face'. I want to be honest with the Lord."

Ernie had to leave immediately after the morning service to make connections for his trip south. After he had gone, Roy said to Gillian: "How good the Lord has been to answer our prayers this way! He's really beginning to revive the Meo church. Let's pray that all may be fully cleansed, and that they may go on from here to *grow*."

"The one who said the least was Simon," Gillian said. "I don't think he came through, although he looked pretty serious and sat with his head down at the meetings."

"We must pray for him specially, Gill. I feel he is a key figure. I think of that verse, 'Simon, Simon, behold, Satan hath desired to have you, that he may sift you as wheat. But I have prayed for thee, that thy faith fail not: and when thou art converted, strengthen thy brethren.' I feel God is yet going to make him into an evangelist."

Early in November, Roy and Gillian were finally free to set out on their trip to Palm Leaf. A strong wind had been blowing for several days. "It looks like the rainy season is over," Roy said, looking up at the clear blue sky and the few fleecy clouds scurrying before the high wind. The dark monsoon clouds were gone; the air crisp and cool. "What a difference to have a dry trail for once," Gillian exclaimed.

At that moment they were startled by an ominous cracking and splintering overhead. "Look out!" Roy shouted as he pulled Gillian off the path. With a crashing descent a giant tree hit the trail only a few feet away, its branches quivering and settling protestingly.

"There are more dangers than we think on the trails, I guess," Roy said shakily, his face pale from their narrow escape. "The ground has been softened by the months of rain and some of these large trees can't take it when these terrific winds blow. It's a shame to see these forest giants die like that, isn't it?" Then he said, more slowly, "but, of course, the death of a giant tree can't be compared with the death of a human. I didn't tell you, Gill, but just before we left the village I heard of another murder. A man and his wife were sleeping the other night when a gunman shot at the side of the bedroom wall. He evidently thought to kill the man who he presumed was sleeping on that side, but the wife was killed instead. Apparently the man owed a large debt, and this was one way of evening the scores in their eyes."

They heard more of this story when they reached Palm Leaf. A Chinese man had just been in to get treatment from Dorothy and Doris for a gunshot wound in his leg.

"That man who was just here was shot at yesterday on the trail," Doris explained. "This is the second attempt on his life. Relatives of the woman who was killed over your way, have been trying to kill the murderer. Somehow they think this Chinese is involved. I don't know if I have the story straight, but two nights ago a man was shot, and they think he was the one who first attempted to kill this Chinese. Now, last night, on the same trail, this Chinese was shot at again."

Doris had scarcely finished her explanation as she and Dorothy prepared the ever-welcome cup of tea for their guests, when a Meo woman came in to ask how the Chinese man who had just left was getting on.

"They are coming to see if he's getting better in a couple of days," Doris explained when she came back in, "and if he is, they'll kill him properly!"

To be living in such an atmosphere of vengeance and violence caused some anxious moments, but the four missionaries were conscious of the Lord's presence with them. They recognized the tension and fears of the people; they did not reckon themselves to be immune to such dangers, but God had given them peace: they were here at His appointment and their times were in His hands.

Roy was cheerfully busy with hammer and saw for the next few days. Dorothy and Doris had a lengthy list of odd jobs they had been saving up for the next man who came by! Roy loved working with his hands. Time for the annual Field Conference was drawing near, however, and he still had his report of the year's work to write. As Gillian was not very well it was agreed that she should remain behind for another twelve days while he returned to Namkhet alone. Dorothy and Doris could accompany her back on their way to Conference. This would be his longest separation from Gillian since they had been married.

These were lonely days for Roy. "It's only a week since I left

Gill at Palm Leaf," he wrote during this time, "but it seems like many more days." Even as he was writing, a Meo lad from Palm Leaf walked in and handed him a note from Gillian. Life with Gill was such fun, he thought. Her cheery note brought her presence right into the room and dispelled some of the loneliness. But some of the news she shared was disturbing. "The Chinese man sleeps alone each night as no one wants to be shot by mistake! The man's in a bit of a state, which I'm sure I would be, too, though he's brought it on himself. They wanted him to come to sleep in our house, and we were glad that we are only girls here so we could say no. They then talked of his going to Namkhet to live with you! They say it's safe to be with the foreigner because foreigners don't get shot. I think the least we have to do with murderers and the murdered the better, or we'll find ourselves and the Lord's work in jeopardy.

"The police arrived today," Gillian had added the next day, "to get the Chinese man. I should think he'll feel safer in prison than alone in the house waiting for the murderer to come and finish him off!"

When the twelve days were up, Roy went along the trail to meet the three from Palm Leaf, with a thermos of cool lime-ade to refresh them. He was glad to find Gillian had made the trip slowly and was feeling much better. However, soon after getting home, she was ill again, this time from spoiled porcupine meat eaten en route. Roy took care of her for the next few days, doing all the cooking. There were delicious carrots, the first from their little garden, a lemon-meringue pie he had made all alone, and also the bread baked successfully! Under this kind of treatment Gillian was soon strong enough to leave for the Conference.

The day before they left, Roy came in from visiting some unbelieving families. "This morning I sensed an overwhelming feeling of hatred against the Lord's message. I've never seen such hardness and hatred directed against me like this before."

He heard later from Mrs. Chieh Shaw that this was the result of reviving elements of the "Meo King" group which had been hidden for almost a year now. Was the whole work going to be upset now? Were the old threats against the lives of the Christians and the missionaries going to begin again? The Lord knew the need of His servants and knew just how to encourage. Roy wrote in his Bible study notes at that time, "The Lord's word to me was II Thessalonians 1.5-12, specially verse 11: 'Wherefore . . . we pray always for you, that our God would count you worthy of this calling, and fulfil all the good pleasure of his goodness, and the work of faith with power.' May our God make us worthy of His call and may He fulfil every good resolve and work of faith by His power. I took this as God's word to my heart when I felt like giving up."

CHAPTER NINE

LAUNCHING INTO THE DEEP

"GOT a surprise for you!" Roy greeted Gillian early one morning in December, after their return from the Annual Conference. Gillian opened the basket he held out to her.

"A darling kitten!" she cried, and cuddled it in her arms.

"Thought I'd better get us a kitten. Rats have done a pretty job on our sheets while we were away. I'm afraid one rat even heard the remark that members of the Mission are to digest the messages of the *Overseas Bulletin*; he did that exactly!"

The kitten settled in her new home. She was named Tweetles, but more often than not was called *Mimi*, the Meo name for cat. Roy shot a rat with his Meo bow and arrow to give her her first lesson. Mimi loved to go on walks with them, and even accompanied them on their days of prayer out at the jungle pool.

One cool December day out at the baptismal pool, Roy built a fire, for high up in the mountains it was penetratingly chilly. "There's one word that has deeply impressed me today," he said to Gillian as he stirred up the fire and added another log. "I've been reading Luke 5.4: 'Launch out into the deep, and let down your nets for a draught.' Oh, Gill, may the Lord keep us from fishing in the shallows and being content with the shrimps and crabs, when He calls for a mightier catch. When Simon obeyed, his nets enveloped a shoal. We little know what harvest God will bring if only we will go deeper and obey."

"I keep thinking of those 'glamour boys' all dressed up for the Meo New Year, who visited us soon after we got back from Conference," Gillian spoke up. "In spite of their being dressed to attract the girls, they really seemed to be interested in the message. Weren't most of them from Tamboe and Dry Creek villages?"

"Yes, I think they were. And you know, since I've been praying about this, I feel we must approach the church about getting out to some of the further villages that have seldom been visited."

Christmas Sunday, December 24, gave Roy the opportunity he had prayed for, to present the message burning on his heart. He had drawn four large Christmas posters and used these to emphasize the fact that outreach to the lost was the heart of the Christmas message. Several of the young men helped Roy with the preaching, also stressing the need to get the Gospel out to the many neglected villages.

On Christmas morning, Roy and Gillian called all the children to come up to their house for a games programme. Roy was surprised how well the children entered into the games, and how much the watching parents enjoyed it all! There were prizes and plenty of balloons, which many of the children had never seen. After the fun was over, Mrs. Chieh Shaw wiped her eyes and said: "I never could laugh and have such fun when we were going the demon way!"

That afternoon each of the Christians brought a small contribution of meat, vegetables and rice, and all partook of a Christmas meal together at Mblia Dua's house. According to good Meo custom, the men were first to sit at the large table. Women filled the children's bowls with the choicest pieces of meat, and they wandered about as they liked while eating. Then when the men were finished, the same bowls and spoons were set out for the women and the serving dishes refilled with steaming meat and vegetables. While they were eating, the men sat round the fire and began to discuss the matter of an evangelistic trip to Tamboe and Dry Creek villages. Roy listened with mounting excitement as they planned, and then decided to leave two days after Christmas—to give Jahu time to butcher a pig. Ying and Jahu were to accompany Roy, and he could have asked for no better team.

Roy got out his new tape recorder and after demonstrating its uses to their delighted exclamations as they each heard his own voice played back, he suggested they record something that could be used on their evangelistic trip. They entered into the novelty and soon had put a simple Gospel message, sung in Meo ballad style, on to the tape.

Jahu took special pains to see that Roy was dressed in proper Meo style before they set out. Quite an audience watched as the brightly embroidered red sash was tied at just the right angle. An old woman peering in at them called to Roy, "Don't you ever wear your foreign clothes again! You must always wear our Meo clothes and be one of us."

Just as they were ready to start out, Mr. Peer, a neighbour, walked in. "Please come and pray for my wife," he asked quickly. "We both want to believe in Jesus and get rid of our spirit things. My wife is very ill, but we still want to do this." Mrs. Peer had had hepatitis and even treatment in the hospital in Pitsanuloke had made no improvement.

"What shall we do?" asked Ying and Jahu.

"I think we had better put off our trip until tomorrow," Ying answered. "We should have a good talk with Peer and his family. We want to be very sure they really believe before they burn their demon things."

After prayer together, they went down to get Mblia Dua to go with them over to the Peer home. Roy was thrilled at the way the men went ahead with everything. All witnessed, one by one, to Mr. Peer about what the Lord had done for them, and what He would do for him and his family. Together they prayed for healing for the sick wife, then told Mr. Peer to think the matter over carefully, and they would see him again when they returned from their evangelistic trip.

Roy, Jahu, and Ying left together the next day for Tamboe. The village seemed deserted when they arrived. But Roy set up his tape recorder, with the Gospel in Meo ballad singing, and soon streams of people began to come from every direction, it seemed, as they heard the typical singing that is so dear to a Meo heart. It amused Roy to see their eyes widen with surprise as the words came from the little box. But they stayed right through to the end of Ying's one-and-a-half-hour sermon!

At Dry Creek village, after playing the tape and Gospel Recordings records, Ying preached to a packed house. Many said, "We never heard the Jesus Way before, and certainly never knew that Meo were keen enough to come to tell us." As Roy settled for the night there, after nearly three hours' witness by Ying and Jahu, he could hear Ying talking far into the night with the head of the house about the Christian life. In the morning, as they set out for home, a number of the villagers came to see them off on the trail, begging them, "Please come back again and visit us soon. We want to hear more about Jesus. Before long all of us will be turning to Jesus." All the way home they talked of the acceptance they had received. Ying and Jahu were elated over the response, and had all manner of ideas for future trips.

"Gill," Roy called when he got home, "we've had a wonderful trip! With a revived church there's a new power in witness among the heathen! Surely the Lord is definitely at work in hearts. When we left, so many told us they were going to believe soon. Pray God they really will!"

As a sombre background for this encouraging interest among the heathen, the spirit of violence continued active in the hills. On January 1st, Roy heard from one of his Meo friends of another murder. "You know those three Thai opium traders? They were robbed and killed the other day, while in the very act of begging for their lives!"

"I wonder if they were those three men who were here only a few days ago," Roy said to Gillian when he was telling her of this report. "The ones we hired to cut our fire-wood. I'm so glad I took the opportunity of telling them of the Lord. But how differently I would have spoken had I known they had only a few days to live!"

January 2nd was a Tuesday and their first day of prayer in the new year. Roy suggested they keep the next day also. What did this year have in store that the Lord burdened him to spend two full days in prayer? The news of the three Thai men had deeply stirred his heart, and he felt more than ever before the urgency to get the message out to dying souls. As was their custom during these days of prayer, Roy shared with Gillian the word he had from the Lord.

"Jude 23 has really hit me," he told her. " 'Save some by *snatching* them *out* of the fire', it is in the marginal reading. We're meant to be aggressive in this business of soul searching! I've been praying today, 'Lord keep us from cold-heartedness and familiarity.' We need to know the fire and know its reality or we'll never be concerned for others. Oh, may I ever trust God alone every time I witness to anyone. It's easier said than done, though!"

They had not forgotten the burden for Mr. Peer. His wife was much better; even able to do a full day's work in the fields! But now that she was better, would they forget the Lord's goodness? Would they remember their resolve?

During the morning service one Sunday later in the month, while Roy was speaking, the whole of the Peer family came in. And at the close of the service, Mr. Peer invited the whole church to come down to his house to help them burn his spirit fetishes! They went down as a group and when the Christians felt that Mr. Peer and his family were determined to follow the Lord, they encouraged him to go ahead and burn his demon things. Roy was thrilled to see the Christians taking this responsibility in questioning, teaching and encouraging these new believers. He said to Gillian, "Honestly, I am amazed at how well they are caring for the Peers; praying with them and just thinking of everything. But we need to pray the Peers through to a complete understanding of the New Birth."

The Enemy's attack came swiftly. Only a day or two after the Peer family had thus publicly confessed the Lord, heathen neighbours came around and demanded payment of a debt. Mr. Peer himself scraped together more than half of the money, and with help from the Namkhet church, the debt was paid.

"These experiences," Roy wrote to friends, "have meant a tremendous lot to the Christians, who seem to have come into their own. They reveal a knowledge of spiritual things which I confess I often wondered if they had. It's made a real impact on the heathen, too, for many others are also contemplating taking the step. Just recently we had two more requests to help some burn their demon things. One request came from Basa's hard village down on the New Road. This place really seems to be softening, with Basa's sister's vigorous witness. We are watching and praying that these may not be just idle words."

A few mornings later Gillian greeted Roy by singing, "*Happy Birthday to You!* It's February 1, you know, and you're twenty-six years old today!" she chanted.

"Well, so I am! I feel much older! Think we could celebrate by having a quiet day at home? We've been on the trail so much these days there's been no time to read and pray together. Sunday and Monday we had the trip to Cawca and back, and Tuesday and Wednesday down to Pitsanuloke to get that letter off to Ernie. Ying and Jahu can't wait on us very much longer, as they need to get their new fields cut and burned off before the rains begin."

"I really don't think you look very well, today, Roy. Perhaps being on the trail four days running has been too much. You carried such a heavy load yesterday. I wish you wouldn't. I know it's because you are concerned about me, but I'm sure we could get along with less."

"What's that I smell burning?" Roy interrupted her.

"My pastry . . ." Gillian wailed as she ran to the oven. "It's burned! And I did so want to have a nice pie for your birthday!"

"Never mind, Gill," Roy laughed. "Here's the tin of thick luscious New Zealand cream we've been saving for some very special occasion. Let's celebrate with this!" And he brought the tin from the store-cupboard in the bedroom.

There was still some of this special treat from home left the next afternoon when Ernie made another of his surprise appearances. "Ernie!" Roy exclaimed as he saw him at the door. "I just wrote you a letter. You couldn't have received it before you left. How did you know we needed you? Now I can tell you everything."

Robin Talbot, a new worker, had come with Ernie, coming

along for the visit, and both men were hungry. Soon Gillian had an early supper ready and the hoarded tin of cream was finally finished as it was lovingly shared with the guests.

"Well, I guess I'd better tell you about that letter," Roy said as they lingered round the table. "It seems the Meo are on the move in earnest this time. Soon Namkhet may cease to be. Maybe this is the Lord's answer to our call for wider evangelism. But the big question is, *Where do we go from here?* Simon and most of the Christians have decided to move to Cawca, but Ying and Jahu are much concerned for the Christians in Bitter Bamboo, though Ying himself feels an increasing burden for the Big Mountain area. Both are afraid that unless one of us goes to live in Bitter Bamboo, they'll soon grow discouraged and probably fall. They asked me to write to you and ask you to consider letting us move over to Bitter Bamboo. Of course, the others want us to go to Cawca!"

"How do you feel about it personally, Roy?" Ernie asked.

"I have no inspiration to go to Cawca," he said slowly, "apart from liking the very convenience of the place! There's a perfect water supply; it's handy to the highway, cool, and when almost all the Christians have moved there, it will be cosy! They want everyone to go with them, and this would be the easy way. Ying and Jahu are fully aware of Bitter Bamboo's disadvantages, for the water supply is awful! And there are other inconveniences; but maybe this is the answer to the prayers of you all who have sought an entrance there for a long time. It will mean building another house; so the Christians wonder if you would discuss the matter with them."

Ernie spent several days in Namkhet, even making a short trip to Cawca. In the meantime, Roy showed Robin life as it was in a Meo village. Since he was one to throw his whole being into whatever task was at hand, it was not unnatural that the first place Roy took Robin was to the little baptismal pool by the mountain stream. "This is our sanctuary," he explained. "Gill and I come out here every week. When I first came up to Namkhet, Robin, I didn't realize that the love I had for these people was just a natural love. It couldn't withstand all the frustrations in store for me. When crowds kept coming and staying so long, and with my little language, I found it very hard to take. I couldn't find any time for Quiet Time. Then, continual disappointments in the Christians made me begin to mistrust all Meo. It was quite a desperate situation until the Lord met me at the time of prayer and fasting in Chiengmai. There He taught me to see Him as being formed in the believers instead of their multitude of little sins. And He also gave me a new love for the Meo and a new faith to expect greater things. It is costing in disciplined prayer, and may cost us everything we've got, but it's worth it. We're beginning to see victories." As Roy told of the battles fought in this place and of the victories won in the presence of the King, a sense of holy hush came upon them.

Returning to the village, Roy took Robin to pound rice for the chickens, and then to see other points of interest: the stone grinder, a woman doing the most intricate embroidery, the water-hole Roy had dug for their use. Finally, as they turned back to the house, there above the dark silhouette of distant ranges was unrolled the breath-taking reminder of the God of Creation—an Eastern sunset. They sat on a log under the eaves of the house gazing out on this scene.

"It reminds me of the verse, 'Remember now thy Creator in the days of thy youth'," Robin said.

"You and I are both young," Roy agreed, "and we need to discharge *to the full* the service He's entrusted to us. One thought that keeps recurring in my reading of Paul's epistles is that of whole-heartedness."

They chatted a long time about the varying needs of their North Thailand field, then, as if he could hold it in no longer, Roy burst out with the great burden on his heart. "How I do long to have a fellow-worker to share the long evangelistic and teaching trips. You know, this next year Dorothy Jones will be home on furlough, leaving Doris alone in Palm Leaf. Gill won't be able to go with me on trips when our baby comes. I'm the only man now in the White Meo work and I do feel so strongly the responsibility weighing upon me." Roy little knew that Robin was at this time interested in another tribe; nor did he have any idea that his words planted the first stirring of a call to the Meo in his heart.

F

In a few days Roy was feeling well enough to set off for Bitter Bamboo with Ernie, Robin, and Ying. He was encouraged to find that Jahu had gone on ahead and was there to talk things over with the little group of Christians, concerning a house for them.

"There's an empty house that you may be able to get," one man suggested. "It belongs to a Meo who killed two Chinese opium traders a few days ago on the trail to Palm Leaf. He's afraid to live here any more and wants to escape into Laos before the police find him. He'd be glad of a chance to sell his house."

But the suggestion was turned down. Apart from its being unwise to get mixed up in a murder case, how could they contact a man continuously hiding in the jungle? It was decided it would be better to build a simple house.

While they were discussing these matters, a man came in quietly and sat down, waiting to deliver his message. "There's a man named Doong who is very ill and wants all of you to come down to help him believe," he said finally when asked. Their discussion was dropped while they hurried down to the man's house to see what they could do. While Ernie and Ying explained the way of salvation, Roy and Robin prayed silently for the miracle of grace to take place in this man's heart. What a thrill to hear him express his clear desire to turn to Christ. Doong had been sick for years, and in spite of his being a spirit *shaman*, his efforts at spirit worship had made no improvement in his health. He was thoroughly disillusioned with the demons, and his heart reached out to Jesus.

"He is greater than the demons, and I want to turn to Him," he said. It was already late in the evening, so they arranged to meet at Doong's the next morning. This would give him time to think the matter through carefully and be certain of his decision.

Roy could scarcely sleep that night. He wondered if Doong was as eager as he for the dawn of a new day, when this great transaction would be settled. Roy rose the next morning at the first light of dawn and with the others made his way prayerfully to Doong's house. As Ernie and Ying made the Gospel very clear, the great moment came. Doong got up from his sick bed and, with the aid of his family, tore down his demon shelf and assortment of fetishes. Being a spirit medium, he had an endless accumulation of jaw-bones from pigs that had been offered to spirits, carved wooden daggers, bowls of rice and popped corn, with sticks of incense. All was made into a bonfire outside for everyone to see; while the food that had been offered to the spirits was greedily consumed by the neighbouring pigs.

"I couldn't have a better seal on our move to Bitter Bamboo than this," Roy said soberly as he said goodbye to Ernie and Robin.

"The decision's made," he greeted Gillian when he got home. "We're definitely moving to Bitter Bamboo." Then he went on to tell her of the seal God had given to their move, and they rejoiced together to have the future step made clear.

But as night settled, troubling thoughts came to nibble at Roy's peace. No one here had time to help in anything. They were all busy making their own fields and houses. How could he get a house built; find horses to move their things? How could he face again having everyone coveting their few belongings, marching into every crevice of their new house and life and sit waiting for meals when they scarcely had enough to eat for themselves.

"Gill," he confessed one morning, "these last few nights I've thought about the move until it's nearly made me ill. The thought of re-living the experience of moving here made me shudder and I've tossed and turned, wishing only for a boat home! Suddenly I woke to the fact this morning that sin was fast getting hold of me. I realized I was shrinking back from the will of God."

"God turned this move to Norgo's house into blessing, and I'm sure He will do the same for us at Bitter Bamboo," Gillian comforted.

"Yes, that's what the Lord showed me. He gave me Psalm 127, 'Except the Lord build the house, they labour in vain. . . . he giveth his beloved sleep.' So I've stopped struggling, Gill. It's His work. I have the assurance that He has an answer for every problem. Now I feel I can honestly say that I look forward to moving over there."

CHAPTER TEN

THE HOUSE IN BITTER BAMBOO

"PEOPLE laughed at me for fussing over watering my plants, but now they're rather envious," Roy said one morning, looking out over the little garden that had been but a quagmire when they moved to Norgo's house. It was unusual to see in late March such a garden with peas, beets, carrots, etc., in Meo-land.

"It's quite an eye-opener to the villagers to see that vegetables can be grown in the hot, dry season," Gillian agreed.

"I think they have the idea of making their own gardens next year. Simon thinks carrots might find a good market to replace opium as a cash crop."

Roy turned back into the little room and got out his writing materials. "Maybe I'd better write about those seeds Simon wants, then I'll go down to the post office and come back by way of Basa's New Road village. Several there have asked me to come; some even say they want to believe."

"Dear Don," he wrote to Don Rulison. "We don't know when Ernie is handing over responsibility, but time for their furlough must be getting close, so I've addressed this to you. Simon and others are very keen to plant a lot of carrots this year for the Pitsanuloke market, and want me to ask you to please send in a big tin of seed! I hope you can do this for me or Simon will chew my ear off, because I've already forgotten to ask once!

"This week-end I went back to Bitter Bamboo to visit the Christians, and found Doong as fit as a fiddle, and looking very smart in a new outfit. It's the talk of the village that he was dying, and only because he turned to the Lord has he been restored. Brother! we're praying it will become real to him and that there'll be no turning back. I confess I move cautiously, knowing past experience.

"Jahu is a joy to worship with. He is still over there making fields, and helped me through the morning service. A little later two fellows came in to see the 'foreigner'. They had just moved in from the north and were very interested. Jahu very simply and sincerely explained the Gospel to them. I was amused when Jahu answered their question: 'How much language does he know?' by politely saying, 'He knows everything'!"

"I'm hoping Doris can plan to stay with us a while when she comes back from her holiday. Then I would feel freer to go across to Bitter Bamboo to get the house going. I could maybe plan to move things across while Gill's waiting in the hospital in Manorom. The Doctor wants her there no later than one month before the baby's due. We'll move when the Meo are ready, not before or later, so I'm trying not to plan too much."

In a few days Roy was back from his trip to the post office. But the snug little shanty with its brave garden looked beaten and ravaged. "What happened?" he cried as Gillian, tired and somewhat dishevelled, came to the door to greet him.

"We had a terrific hailstorm last night," she said, relief lighting her face that Roy was here to deal with things. "I was rushing around trying to keep things dry when huge hailstones began to crash through the windows. And then the roof started to give way, and I gave up!"

Together, they soon had bedding and books outside to dry. As they worked, Gillian asked about his visit to Basa's village.

"It seemed a fruitless visit," Roy answered as he arranged the books on a nearby log to air. "There was scarcely any freedom in Basa's house to preach. Most of the people who said they wanted to believe didn't come anywhere near me! That night Basa brought out a letter sent to him from his son, Bow, in prison in Bangkok."

"He's the one convicted of murder a few years ago, isn't he?"

"Yes, that's the fellow. You know, he really seems to believe now. One of Basa's other sons read the letter for all the household to hear, and it seemed all through the letter he was saying over and over again, 'Believe in the Lord Jesus and be saved, for there is only one way'. Basa was obviously not pleased and decided there and then that he would leave for Bangkok the next day to visit Bow. He got me to look through all his gun licences, for he wanted to take his big pistol in case of robbers.

We spent until midnight looking through the pile, for he has half a dozen guns, it seems."

"What a job to be doing when you could have been talking to those who wanted to turn to the Lord," Gillian sympathized as Roy helped her hang up a damp blanket.

"While we were going through the licences, Basa told me about a man from a Thai village somewhere near kilometre 80 on the New Road, who cleverly stole a gun from one of the Meo. This Meo was taking his gun into town to be repaired when the Thai 'friend' accompanied him to the shop. Later, the Thai went back to pick up the repaired weapon, 'for my Meo friend', he said, and disappeared. When the Meo came for his gun, it was too late. Basa's really afraid of those men. 'That whole village is a bunch of robbers,' he said. He doesn't like them living so close.

"The next morning about 5, I heard Basa doing some demon worship, and when I went out he was looking at the bones of the chicken he'd killed, to see if the demons would let him go to Bangkok. He said the demons said, 'No'. But I feel the Lord stopped him, for his intentions were not good."

Everything dried out that day and Roy mended the roof temporarily. It was not much use doing a proper repair job as they would be leaving in a few weeks. "The sooner we move now the better!" was Roy's feeling.

Early in April, Roy dashed into the house from a visit in the village. "Gill," he called, "Jahu's gone back to Bitter Bamboo today. He says that when they've planted their corn they will probably cut leaves for their house and ours!"

"Wonderful!" exclaimed Gillian. "To think our house is actually getting started!"

"I'm going over this Thursday to see about getting boards cut for the walls. I want to take over a couple of horse-loads of things, too. I'm sure I can store them in Zay's house for the time being. I've been given the use of two horses."

"So the move's begun!"

"But there's one thing that bothers me," Roy continued. "Jahu says that the believers over there are willing to help, but the motive is money. If I yield to their wishes the house will be quite costly. I made it clear to him that if no one is willing to lend a hand without expecting to be generously paid, then we wouldn't go at all!"

"The group there's a pretty poor lot, with only backslidden believers to be an example to the new ones. It would be no help to them if we encouraged their covetousness," Gillian agreed.

"My natural feelings are to go ahead and get a house up quickly, but I don't think it would be of any lasting value to anyone if they were only satisfied in the natural."

Over at Bitter Bamboo, Roy heard the disturbing rumours that thieves had again broken into the missionaries' house in Palm Leaf, and had stolen everything including boards off the walls and grass from the roof. Feeling strongly that he should go over and investigate, he set out immediately.

When he came to the two mammoth rocks, *The Dragon* and *The Tiger*, somehow the sight of them depressed him. As on so many previous occasions on these lonely trails, he wished for another fellow-worker. As the only man in the White Meo work, the responsibilities weighed heavily upon him. The darkness of the wild, tangled jungle did not help to lift his spirits. It only seemed to emphasize the spiritual darkness around him. The wicked act of vandalism in the home of the two brave women depressed him further.

As his eyes dropped from the two outstanding boulders, with their gruesome legends, he started. *What was that by the trail?* Something lay hidden in the vines. He stepped aside to investigate and stiffened with horror and revulsion as he looked down on the bodies of two men, already decaying and beyond description, lying half-hidden in the tangled underbrush. Then he remembered. It had been reported that two Chinese traders had been murdered along this trail two months ago. These undoubtedly were the bodies of the two.

For the first time, icy fingers of personal fear clutched at his heart. He could not shake it off, or rid his mind of the terrifying thoughts that rushed in upon him. It could happen to him. What would become of Gill and the baby if he were shot? He moved on, but vigorous walking did not wholly rid him of the strange

At Any Cost

paralysing dread that had gripped him at this fresh reminder of the violence and lawlessness loose in these hills.

Doris was not at home, but the house was still standing. He made a thorough inspection. Pigs had ruined the garden, and at one side of the house wall boards had been removed. He crawled through the hole into the house, but it was hard to tell how much had been stolen as he knew that Dorothy and Doris now stored some things in Doong Ye's house when they were away. Roy went to find Mrs. Doong Ye, and the story was gradually pieced together.

Apparently, self-appointed Thai "officials" for unknown reasons had chopped a hole in the wall of the missionaries' house to make an "investigation". Afterwards anyone else who wanted to take anything could just walk in. It looked as though a great many had been in and had had a gay time. Roy was thoroughly displeased and said to Mrs. Doong Ye, "If this happens again, I don't think Doris will be allowed back here to live. I think it's the responsibility of you Christians to look after the house."

Roy spent the night in Doong Ye's house, but sleep was long in coming. A cloud of depression engulfed him and he could not forget the sight of the dead men under the jungle vines. In agony he cried to the Lord, and into his heart there stole His answer from II Corinthians 10.5, "Bringing into captivity every thought to the obedience of Christ." Gratefully he clung to this promise and sleep came.

It was not very pleasant telling Gillian the story when he returned to Namkhet. "I had no peace waking or sleeping until I remembered II Corinthians 10.5. What havoc uncontrolled thought can play!"

"I know, Roy," Gillian confessed. "Often when you've been away on a trip and haven't come home when I expected you, all kinds of thoughts have panicked me—till I remembered to look to Him. It is wonderful how the Lord gives peace, then."

"Well, I think we need to face it," Roy said quietly. "It doesn't seem to matter whether there are one or two or even three together on the trail; they still can be killed. We never know what will happen. This makes eight murders since we returned from Chiengmai in September. But we *do* know we are completely in the Master's hand to do with us what He pleases."

April 8 was the last Sunday before the Namkhet church scattered in several directions. The majority were moving to Cawca where they had already cleared new fields. It was a memorable day, full of blessing, and the presence of the Lord was in the three services. The house was full that morning as everyone realized it would be a farewell service. Roy was specially glad to see Simon come for the first time in weeks. He had been gambling again and had been getting farther and farther from the Lord. Roy felt God used the message Ying gave that morning to speak directly to Simon's heart.

Everyone was present that afternoon for the Lord's Supper, even Nzoe whose hurt feelings had kept him away for so long. It was a special joy to welcome him back to the fellowship of the group, after adequate evidence of repentance was given. At the end of the meeting, Roy brought out the box of church offerings and suggested that its contents be disposed of and that at each of the new places they could start over again. The result was an added blessing to see the church decide to give the money to outside causes. Half was set aside for leprosy work in Central Thailand, and half to Gospel broadcasting, specially for Thai and Meo programmes. Since the Meo broadcasts from Laos had begun, many had been coming in to listen to the radio and Jahu especially was thrilled with excitement over this new way of hearing about the Lord.

"I think this was a major victory for them," Roy said later to Gillian. "To think that they have grown spiritually enough to see that they ought not always to use the money on their own local needs!"

That evening there was another major step taken when, at a little consecration service, Ying and Leah were set aside as the representatives of Christ and His Church to the Big Mountain area. Ying had just returned after a two months' absence in Big Mountain to make fields and build their house. The Big Mountain area had long been a burden on his heart and when Jahu and Mrs. Chieh Shaw had agreed to move to Bitter Bamboo with Roy and Gillian, Ying and Leah had felt free to go. It was no easy decision—they knew they would face hardships in moving to a new area where there were no close relatives to help with fields and with building a house. Big Mountain was reputed to be an area with bands of robbers, difficult trails and distant from any town. Being a semi-nomadic people, these difficulties did not loom too largely in the minds of this eager young couple. But what about Christian fellowship? That was what made the decision a difficult one. No fellow believers with whom to worship and pray; no sharing of thoughts from the Word. No one with whom to try out new hymns or any of the other joys which had almost automatically become part of the life since they first turned to the Lord. But their growing conviction that this was what God wanted them to do, settled the issue.

The little ceremony for Ying and Leah also reminded all the believers that wherever they went, they were God's representatives and must bear witness to that fact.

Two days later, Roy and Gillian were delighted to hear Doris's familiar voice calling as she neared their shanty. "I can stay to be lady-in-waiting till Gill goes to Manorom," she said cheerfully as she came in. "Here's all your mail. There was a lot of it accumulated in Pitsanuloke and it looked as if you'd not had mail for a long time, so I brought it all up. How's the house coming?"

"But you shouldn't have carried such a load," Roy protested.

"Never mind . . . but go on! I want to hear all about your new house!"

"It's well under way now. Zay has matters in hand. Boards are already being cut, and leaves will be ready in a week, he says. Now that you're here to be with Gill, I'll be able to stay over there and get the house up so that we can take our things across as soon as I return from taking Gill down to the hospital. I don't want to leave this home alone longer than I have to, as there are so few Christians left in the village."

Roy was away a good deal in the following days, spending all the time he could in Bitter Bamboo. Whenever he came back to Namkhet he would be bombarded with questions from Doris and Gillian who wanted to know all the details.

"The framework is just about ready to go up, but it's been an exhausting job getting the boards ready. The Bible has so much to say about waiting on the Lord, but I must confess I find it hard to be patient at times. When I found a lot of the boards cut too short, I frankly didn't know what to do, so I asked the Lord about it. Really, I felt like leaving the place, with no one willing to help other than Jahu and Nia Bow. But I knew it was His will to go on. Jahu couldn't have done more to help, considering he has his own house to build as well. Zay is such an opium sot he hasn't been much help at all."

"Where have you been staying?"

"At Zay's house. It's quite an experience! At night the house is turned into an opium den, and often four or five men are lying about smoking until three in the morning. But in spite of this, I believe the Lord is working in several hearts over there. Many of the heathen are definitely weary of serving the demons and are wanting to know more of the Lord."

"Have they given you much to eat? You look thinner," Gillian asked anxiously.

"Well, they don't have much during the dry season, but they share what they have. Just rice and wild vegetables most of the time. It's very exhausting doing heavy work on such a diet. I carried nearly all the boards myself. They were cut at the bottom of a waterfall, and after I'd carried them all to the top and fallen over a few times, I decided to pay someone to carry them on to the house! I wish I could talk over these problems with Don Rulison. I hated to add to the agreed cost of the house. But I guess the Lord wanted me to shoulder the responsibility alone. 'Bewildered, we are never at our wits' end', as the New English Bible renders II Corinthians 4.9, and I'm finding it is true."

Roy was soon gone again and was not home for their wedding anniversary on April 27. However, on the 28th he made his way over to Namkhet. Wild flowers, revived by the first rains, grew hidden along the trail. Roy loved the jungle and its wild beauty. It was a shame that such grand stately trees, the sanctuary of birds and wild life, and delicate flowers such as these were so ruthlessly cut down and burned over to make new fields. At one place where the trail led across one such burned-over patch,

Roy stopped in delight to see that beautiful little ground orchids had pushed their way through the ashes and were blooming in gay abandon on this very scene of death. Their message went straight to his heart. The previous Sunday had been Easter Sunday, and now these orchids made the presence of the resurrected Lord very real to him there on the burned hillside. He stooped and gathered a few to take to Gillian. Nearing Namkhet, just at the turn of the trail, he met Gillian and Doris. "How did you know I was coming?" he asked delightedly.

"I don't know," Gillian answered. "But I had a feeling you'd be coming today."

"Here's my gift to you for our wedding anniversary," he said softly.

"Oh, thank you, Roy," Gillian exclaimed, her face lighting with pleasure and appreciation of the beauty of the flowers and his remembrance of their day.

That night as they climbed on to their bed-platform and sat for a while as was their custom to review the Lord's working or Word, they began to think aloud together over the year just past, their first year of marriage. The anniversary alone would have been occasion enough for this; in another sense it was a farewell ritual for this little home, and preparation for new steps ahead.

"I suppose everyone thinks their marriage is something extra special," Gillian observed. "Ours certainly is!"

"Nothing on earth could be sweeter than our love; highlighted as it is by the difficulties of Meo village life," Roy agreed contentedly.

"Our life together in this little home has been all sweetness and purity, and such fun! Remember Christmas Day, our first Christmas as Mr. and Mrs. Orpin! It was lovely! Better than any presents."

"I remember those mincemeat pies, and taking them piping hot, with a lamp and a stool, out of the village to eat in the jungle!" Roy recalled.

"And the funny things you did sometimes! Taking my plate from under my nose while saying grace . . . letting Mimi sleep in your jacket during breakfast . . . diving into bed head first.

There's never been a cloud between us. This may have been about the hardest year of our lives in some ways, but I know one thing—*it has been the happiest*!"

"Well, we surely have a wonderful year to look back on," Roy agreed, "and lots more to look forward to, if the Lord wills."

The next two days were full of preparations for taking Gillian down to the hospital. Doris was going to escort her all the way to Manorom hospital, but Roy was going as far as Pitsanuloke. He wanted to return to Namkhet to finalize the moving. The little house in Bitter Bamboo was now finished, and there only remained the making of the dining-room table, doors, bed and garden fence.

That last evening Roy took Gillian out for a walk. "I guess this will be our last walk together in Namkhet," he said.

"Yes," she agreed. "The village is almost gone and we will be living in Bitter Bamboo afterwards. These next few weeks are not going to be easy for you."

"For some strange reason," Roy answered slowly, "the Lord seems to keep giving me Luke 21.34-36 over and over again. I realize I must be careful lest my heart is weighed down with the cares of this life. . . . Then I've been reading in Mark where Jesus was walking on the water. He said, 'Take heart, it is I, have no fear.' These are just some of the verses the Lord has given me lately."

"They're good verses to keep in mind during these next few weeks," Gillian answered.

"Let's decide what to call the baby," he suggested tenderly. "We might not be able to have another talk like this before Junior arrives! There's one name I like, I think, better than any others. It's a boy's name," he laughed, "guess I'm planning on a son! It's Murray."

That night Roy poured out his heart to the Lord for his Gill. He had an odd feeling in his heart that he might not be with her when the baby was born. It was not always possible to plan travel in the mountains during the rainy season. He prayed that God would give her special joy in having the baby and that His blessing should rest on this new little life that was being entrusted to them.

"Looks like the rainy season's settled in," Roy said dubiously next morning as they prepared to set off. The trail was slippery, but they took their time and by late afternoon they were nearing the New Road village.

"I guess we'll make it after all," Doris said encouragingly, "but Gill looks pretty tired. Maybe we ought to rest a bit at the village."

Basa's mother met them at the edge of the village and welcomed them warmly. "Oh, come to my house and make yourselves comfortable," she insisted. "You can't go by without stopping!

"I and my youngest son want to burn our demon fetishes," she went on as soon as they were seated comfortably in her shanty. "We really want to return to the Lord. I've never been happy since Basa forced us back to the demons. We'd like to do it today while you're here, but all the family is not at home."

"I'll be back soon," Roy assured her, "and then you can do it all together."

Cheered by this token of the hunger of a heart, the three continued on to a hotel in Pitsanuloke. Early next morning, Roy would return to the hills while Doris and Gillian would catch the train south en route for the Christian hospital in Manorom. His Gill was in good hands and safely down the mountain. He could now concentrate on getting the house ready before the heavy rains set in and made the mountain trails almost impassable. They were to have their yearly holiday after the baby came, and there would be no time then to do odd jobs and lay in stores for the four months of rainy season. And so he returned to Bitter Bamboo, his heart at rest, but with quite a heavy load of nails, locks and things for the new house.

On Sunday evening, May 13, Roy sat at the sturdy little dining-table he had recently finished and wrote to Don Rulison, recounting some of the events of the days just past and something of the plans ahead.

"I'm planning to be on the plains on Tuesday to get stores at Pitsanuloke and bring them up here before finally leaving for Manorom on Friday to be with Gill. Since you folk at Chiengmai have been praying about our move to Bitter Bamboo, I am writing this to let you know how things are progressing.

"Last Wednesday week I arrived back in Namkhet to stay up half the night to finalize packing, and on Thursday morning got away with four horse-loads and seven folk carrying clumsy articles. It was a tremendous relief to see the things on the move. The men and horses went before, and I made up the rear to make sure all was well. I was accompanied by our little black kitten, Mimi. She is the cutest thing, with a mind of her own, determined to trot along in the rear and not be carried.

"When about 1½ hours out of Namkhet, the poor little thing ran into trouble. I wondered what the red things stuck to her were, when she abruptly ran off into the jungle. She had run into a wasps' nest! Suddenly I, too, was covered from head to foot with the wretched things. All who had gone before had been stung, yet not one stopped to tell those on the trail behind that the wasps were there! I immediately began to swell up like a balloon! Obviously this was no time to start looking for the cat, so I struggled on to Bitter Bamboo. I was burning from head to toe and wondered if I'd ever make it, all the time encouraged by the 'brethren' who thought it was the greatest joke seeing me all swollen! When I arrived, I told Jahu and his family what had happened. Knowing how much we appreciated the cat, he asked the carriers to look out for her on their return trip. He was much concerned over my wasp stings, and early the next morning came calling through the boards of the bedroom to see if I was all right.

"As soon as everyone realized I'd come, those with ancient and modern sicknesses came from dawn till dark for help. I've tried desperately to get all the work done, respond to their spiritual and physical calls, and prepare my own meals. It's been almost impossible. The last couple of days I've felt myself almost driven beyond endurance, and wanting to put all the 'social callers' out of the house! Perhaps one is meant to get into desperate positions like this to know one's weaknesses. I have had to depend continually upon Christ and claim the fulfilling of His purposes for this place, for I feel myself going under with the strain.

"Jahu and his family have been a blessing to live beside. They witness to everyone who comes to visit them. There is no mincing of matters as they unashamedly tell of the Lord. When Jahu is present and an opportunity comes to speak to someone of Christ, I just give him the lead and let him go ahead.

"The other morning I was planning to go over to Palm Leaf to get the house ready for Doris and carry her things down from Doong Ye's house. I didn't know who would be coming with her, but thought it might be one of the new workers. Just before I set out, a Mr. Do came and wanted me to get some of the Christians to go burn his demon things! He and his father, who is Doong Ye's elder brother, both wanted to believe. The father listened well as we witnessed to him, but I wasn't sure how much Mr. Do's heart was in it, as he didn't stay to watch the burning. None the less, Doong Ye was thrilled when I told him about it later, as you can imagine.

"I finally got to Palm Leaf last Tuesday and found, to my dismay, that the house had been ransacked even more than before. The front locks had been chopped off and the boards in the small back bedroom levered off. It was obvious that the object was vandalism, as tracts were strewn about, the windows were smashed, and a general mess everywhere. Some of the books were soaked through from the rain.

"I immediately set to, to clean it up. I think the very fact of our returning there must be the strongest rebuke to the people living in the place. I did some straight talking to those who came asking for medicine, and told them plainly that this was the final year if they didn't believe!

"The first job was to screw a lock back on the front door, and put plastic sheets into the gaping holes in the roof to try to protect the books from further damage from the coming thunderstorm. The roof is absolutely shocking, and I only wish I were free to get the place back into living order. Goats had been in the garden and eaten absolutely everything. Pigs were sleeping on the back porch.

"I put the matter straightly to Doong Ye, who admitted he hadn't been near the house. When I left, he couldn't have offered to be of more help to the ladies, who by then had returned. When he was over here the other day, the Christians got on to him and asked him why he hadn't previously been more helpful! I think he felt a little ashamed of himself when he left here. It was all done in love and grace, but was needful.

"The first rainstorm after the ladies' arrival soaked their beds through. The water literally poured through the leaf roof. I was able to repair it a little more before I left, but by no means perfectly. But what impression life in a Meo village made on Celia,[1] I don't know.

"The Christians in Big Mountain, Cawca, and New Road villages are all asking for resident missionaries. How long should we maintain Palm Leaf station when its people are so unyielding to Christ? Since I cannot possibly fit in another trip to New Road, I have asked Simon to take Sing with him, and go and help them burn their demon things.

"I plan to arrive in Manorom to be with Gill on Saturday, the 19th. After that I hope to catch up on some much needed Meo study before we make our way to Chiengmai and our holiday in early June. I feel at present I could do with a four *months'* holiday, not just four weeks!

"*When are the White Meo going to get another male worker?* I confess that I need a recommissioning every time I set out on these trails alone. Why is it so hard to get even one carrier, let alone another fellow-worker?

"Incidentally, a Meo brought Mimi over from Namkhet. She had gone back there. He said, 'I knew you loved her'.

"Warmest greetings in the Lord to you all,

"Roy.

"P.S. The oldest living Meo—they say she was 100 or more—died several days ago and there has been a horrible commotion going on two houses away, night and day, ever since. Crowds have flocked into our house continually. We had over sixty to the morning service, where I tried hard—with Mrs. Chieh Shaw's and Jahu's help—to speak on *Death as God sees it*. We all feel a fruitful witness was borne."

Roy folded the letter and put it into an envelope. "Mrs. Chieh Shaw was such a help today," he mused. "I'm sure the memory of her husband's radiant face when he came to die made the

[1] Celia Glass, now Mrs. Robin Talbot.

message very real to her." He looked over the notes he had made on John 5.19-29 that morning, and the simple questions he had asked: *What is death? Why death? Can we escape it? When will it come? Should we fear it? What happens immediately after? What is the future hope for us?*

"Lord, help these people to remember this word," he prayed. "Make it burn within their hearts and turn them to Thee. And keep my heart ever burning with concern for these dying souls. Keep it ever fresh before me lest I forget or grow cold."

CHAPTER ELEVEN

NOT LEFT TO DIE

ACCORDING to plan, Roy loaded his stores on to the eight o'clock bus in Pitsanuloke, on Wednesday morning. This was his last trip before he would be joining Gillian. His heart leapt at the thought. This feeling of elation remained with him as the bus sped down the new highway. The Lord had helped him to complete everything so that he was away in good time.

They were just six kilometres short of his destination, when the bus slowed to pick up more passengers. Three men got on and Roy noticed them largely because they looked so unkempt and disreputable. "Yet they're so young," he murmured. Two were barely in their twenties and one a little older. The young Thai were usually so spick and span in their appearance and cleanliness. His glance fell on the kilometre marker they were just passing, kilometre 80, and he suddenly remembered Basa's story. "Maybe they are after more Meo guns," he thought grimly.

As the bus slowed for his stop at kilometre 86, he noted with satisfaction the dozen or so young Meo, with the seven horses as promised. All was going according to schedule. The bus stopped with a jolt and a squeal of brakes and Roy swung off. He wondered briefly why the three Thai men also got off; they had ridden a very short distance. He saw them start for the first or the two little shacks as he gave his attention to getting his stores unloaded. Then he went along to the second shack as most of the Meo seemed to be there.

"It's too bad none of the Christians came. I'd have enjoyed their company on the trail," he thought, looking over the group of young lads who had come to meet him. As he sat down on a low stool, he noticed the Thai boy who lived here with his mother who sold bananas and rice to travellers.

Roy reached into his pocket and pulled out a gaily coloured children's tract and handed it to the lad.

"I don't know how to read," the boy replied shyly.

"Come here, then, and I'll read it to you," Roy invited, with a smile that put the lad at ease. "This story is about a wonderful Person named Jesus," he began, and read the story through. When he had finished, he looked at his watch and saw it was almost 11. The Meo lads were nearly finished with the loads.

"I'll change into my shorts for the trail," he decided. "I don't want them to have to wait for me." He shouldered his pack and started across the highway towards the beginning of the trail.

"Don't start ahead by yourself," called one of the boys. "Wait a minute and we'll all go together."

"I'm only going a little way to change my clothes," he called back, and began to climb the crude steps that had been cut in the steep embankment to help travellers reach the trail on the level above. He had just finished changing when he heard someone coming. He moved from behind the clump of bamboo just as the three Thai men stepped on to the trail. Guns levelled directly at him left no doubt as to their threat or purpose. It all seemed a bit unreal, but Roy had time to realize and marvel at his lack of fear and the quiet peace flooding his heart.

"Hand over your valuables!" the older man called roughly. Roy calmly took out his wallet with its 500 *baht*[1] and handed that to him. Then he removed his wristwatch, reached into his pocket for his fountain-pen, and gave those to the men. They certainly had him at a disadvantage and there seemed nothing else to do.

"All right, go on!" they ordered gruffly, and motioned him

[1] Approx. £8 15s.

on up the trail. Roy turned, but he had taken only a few steps when there was a crash of sound in his ears and a simultaneous searing, stabbing pain in his neck and lower back.

"This is it," swift knowledge poured through him, as he stumbled and fell. "O, Lord! Take care of Gill!" he cried.

It was very quiet on the trail as he lay there, still conscious. The robbers had not waited to make certain he was dead, but had fled quickly through the trees. But why didn't someone come? Where were the Meo? They could not fail to have heard the shots. Why didn't they come?

At last he heard a soft step on the trail and saw through the mists of his faintness the young Thai lad to whom he had been reading. "Tell the Meo to come and help me," he whispered painfully. The boy ran off, but the Meo did not come. It was their fear of evil spirits, he realized. They were not Christian lads.

Waves of blackness engulfed him again and again, but at one point when he had regained consciousness he began to wonder if he could get himself up and back down the trail. He had struggled to a crouching position when he heard voices. Soon he saw a Thai bus inspector, leading a group of the Meo, reach the trail.

"Carry him to the bus," the inspector ordered quickly. And to the bus driver a few moments later, "Get to the hospital in Pitsanuloke as fast as you can! Don't stop for anyone along the way."

"Thank you, Lord," Roy murmured and lapsed into unconsciousness again.

The bus driver obeyed orders and drove rapidly for the hospital. He was taking a grave risk. He was a Buddhist, and according to Buddhist beliefs, if Roy had died in the bus it would have been defiled. But he obeyed orders and at 1.30 p.m. pulled in to a stop in the grounds of the Pitsanuloke Government Hospital, where swift and experienced nurses and doctors took over.

"I'm still alive!" Roy said with weak amazement as he came back to the present to find himself being wheeled along the corridors of the hospital. "And someone here speaks English!" he exclaimed with relief as a nurse asked his name. He was glad he did not have to think in either Thai or Meo just now. Miss Fiesel, a Canadian nurse serving with the World Health Organization and attached to this hospital only temporarily, stayed with him through the four hours he was on the operating table, and later continued to give him special nursing care. It was she who saw that a telegram was sent to Don Rulison in Chiengmai.

When Don, accompanied by Arnold and Evelyn Melbourne —Evelyn to help with the nursing if needed—arrived about 2 a.m. they found Roy resting as comfortably as possible, though he was still in a critical condition. They learned then of the extent of his injuries and the care he had received; how he had been brought to the hospital in the shortest time possible, and had received skilled care such as he could have found in no other place in that area. He had lost a large quantity of blood on the trail, and had needed three pints when he was being prepared for surgery and five more pints afterwards. Very few places outside Bangkok would have had a blood bank. Miss Fiesel told them that from the medical standpoint it was the skilled anaesthetist who had kept Roy alive through the surgery. The surgeon, too, had had much experience with such extensive internal damages, and everything possible, anywhere, had been done for Roy.

They found him in a large 30-40 bed ward, and seven other gunshot cases there were mute evidence of the violence in the area. How good it seemed to Roy to wake to find familiar faces around him, and to learn that Gillian had been informed of the accident and was on the way.

Gillian arrived about midnight on Thursday. Roy had been quite critically ill all day, but had rallied and was conscious again when she came. His face lighted with joy as he saw Gillian bending over him. "How did you come?" he asked.

"By the Manorom landrover."

"Who is with you?"

"Natalie Ray." He recognized Natalie just behind Gillian, then. She had been Gillian's American room-mate in the Language Centre.

"Has the baby come yet?"

"No," Gillian assured him.

"Oh, good! Then maybe there'll be time to get back to Manorom after all! But, Gill," he asked anxiously, "are you all right? Was the news a terrible shock to you?"

"Not as much as it would have been if the Lord had not prepared me, Roy," Gillian answered softly. "In my reading this morning my attention was suddenly focused on these words: 'He shall not be afraid of evil tidings: his heart is fixed, trusting in the Lord.' When, about midday, the telegram came to say you were in Pitsanuloke hospital with serious gunshot wounds, I knew why the Lord had given me that verse in the morning."

"How good He is," Roy whispered.

The news of Roy's accident travelled swiftly through the mountains to the Meo villages. They were stunned. Mrs. Chieh Shaw's letter, sent to him by one of the four young men who came down the mountain immediately, expressed something of their shock and concern.

Teacher Roy:

Why have you met such trouble as this? I am concerned for you. You are in deep trouble and pain. I heard you were seriously hurt. You are in great bitterness. My heart hurts very much for you. Tears keep coming. I think that if your health returns, and your strength returns, we will probably be able to talk together of your trial. I cannot come to visit you. Though you do not see us coming, know that we love you. Although my heart cares for you, I cannot do anything to heal your body, even a little bit.

If, after your sickness is healed you do not return, never mind. If you abandon your house here, I will see it every day and grieve for you. I will not stop longing for you till your house and garden gets old and decays. I do not know how many times I will weep before my tears will stop.

Mother Chieh Shaw.

When the four Meo had come to enquire after Roy on Friday afternoon, he had taken a turn for the worse, but by evening he had rallied again and they were allowed to see him for a few minutes. As they talked, Roy turned to Simon and with deep feeling in his voice said, "Simon, remember the Lord Jesus." Simon, usually gay and talkative, was suddenly speechless, pierced to his heart. He knew, better than anyone else, that he had not always remembered the Lord and even now was following afar off. . . .

"It's wonderful to be alive!" Roy greeted Gillian and Natalie when they came into the ward early Saturday morning. He had had a better night; much of the restlessness was gone and he even looked refreshed. He reached for Gillian's hand as she sat down by the bed and then flashed a smile to Natalie, too. She was God's provision for Gill at this time, he thought, just the friend that she needed.

"Are you all right?" he asked again, his eyes hungrily on Gillian's face.

"I'm fine, Roy," she answered softly. "Natalie here sees that I rest when I should and eat when I should. I'm being taken care of like a baby!" She laughed and added, "It's for our baby's sake, of course."

His eyes lighted and he smiled contentedly. Then Gillian began to tell him of the lovely little cottage they had been given in the hospital grounds—just a few steps from his ward—the nicest of the ones prepared as private quarters for convalescent patients and their families. "And from our window we can see the maternity wing of the hospital—it is a beautiful modern building. So, if the baby *should* come while we are here," she laughed softly, "I'd only have to walk a few steps to get there. And best of all, we can move you over to our little cottage just as soon as you can eat more and are a little stronger. . . ."

"Couldn't we move over tonight?" he asked eagerly. "I'd like that—I really don't want to spend another night here."

"We'll see," she promised softly.

A little later he said: "Gill, would you say for me the chorus of 'Jesus! I am resting, resting'?" Steadily, Gillian began:

> "Jesus! I am resting, resting
> In the joy of what Thou art;
> I am finding out the greatness
> Of Thy loving heart."

"How good He is," Roy whispered again. How good it was to rest in the everlasting arms of his heavenly Father. He smiled and closed his eyes, and before long was sleeping quietly.

"It's wonderful, Gill," Natalie said, "to see him resting so much better. Yesterday I was afraid of internal bleeding as he was so restless. But that seems almost gone now."

"Yes," Gill answered slowly. But she was remembering the word she had read this morning before coming in to Roy. "Precious in the sight of the Lord is the death of his saints", and then, "I shall not die, but live, and declare the works of the Lord". What was God trying to tell her?

Then, as she sat quietly by Roy's bedside, it seemed the Lord spoke directly to her. "Are you willing if I should take him?"

Through suddenly stiff lips, she whispered, "Not my will, but Thine, Lord." Then choking, she buried her face in her hands and sat unmoving by Roy's bed as he slept.

CHAPTER TWELVE

DAWN OF HARVEST

THROUGHOUT that Saturday, Roy seemed to be resting. He slept for short periods of time, then would wake to rest contentedly in Gillian's presence. But towards evening he began to lapse again into unconsciousness. Gillian and Natalie were with him, but when Evelyn came to relieve them for supper they went quickly so that they could return soon. Roy had had these lapses frequently, but had rallied from each and seemed stronger each time.

But while they were eating, Evelyn came to call Natalie. "I just don't like the looks of things," she said. "I wish you'd come and see what you think."

"Gill," Natalie said swiftly. "I'll go over and see how things are and then I'll come back and tell you. Wait here for me, please, and go on with your supper if you can. Remember, it is for the baby, too."

"All right," Gillian said steadily. "I'll wait." Natalie hurried off, grateful that Gillian was functioning more as a wife than a nurse momentarily. She did not seem to realize the significance of failure at this time. In a little while she was back. She slipped in and put her arm round Gillian as she said: "Gill, darling, the doctor was in and he says there is a renal shut-down; his kidneys have failed."

Gillian's already pale face whitened. "Is there anything they can do?" she whispered.

"No, medically speaking, there isn't," Natalie answered tenderly.

"How long does it take?" she asked, her voice strained and unnatural.

"It's usually just a matter of a few hours," Natalie answered steadily. In any other circumstances Gillian would have known this; her mind was stunned now by the implications.

Suddenly, she seemed to take on new stature as her shoulders straightened and her face lifted. " 'It is the Lord: let him do what seemeth him good'," she quoted softly, and hurried out after Natalie.

At 10.15 that night Roy passed quietly into the presence of his heavenly Father in whose everlasting arms he had been resting.

"This morning," Gillian said steadily, when she knew Roy had gone, "I felt God ask me, 'Are you willing if I should take him?' And though I never really thought He would, He enabled me to say, 'Not my will, but Thine.' God meant it; but He also gave me the wonderful promise in Psalm 118.17, 'I shall not die, but live, and declare the works of the Lord'. It's just like John Deane, principal of our Bible School, said. 'One of these days you'll hear that John Deane has died. Don't you believe it! I'll be more alive then than I ever was before!' It's like that for Roy, I know. He wasn't able to move across to our little cottage here as he wanted to, and he didn't manage to take us back to the mountain home he had worked so hard to prepare, but he has gone instead to his Father's House to spend the night, *no*, the *eternal day* in the mansion which the Lord Jesus went ahead to prepare for him!"

The Thai Christians in Pitsanuloke wanted the privilege of arranging the funeral, and they also asked if they might take care of all the expense. So Gillian did not have to be concerned with any of the arrangements or responsibility. The funeral was held on Sunday afternoon, May 20, attended by many Thai Christians, who rallied to express their love and sympathy. Only a few of the Meo friends could be there. They looked stricken and lost. Gillian, calm and dry-eyed now, watched as they lowered the coffin into the grave, and whispered, "It is not Roy that is being buried here; it is only his body—the shell. He is with the Lord and one day we'll meet again. How wonderful that I have his baby!"

Later she spoke of the tender way the Lord was continuing to uphold and sustain her. "It was just eight weeks ago yesterday that we had the funeral service for Roy. Last year we were married, all we could think of was that we had stretching out before us many wonderful years of service together for the Lord. And yet, it was His will that Roy had only one year to spend among the Meo. But the Lord knew, too, that he needed a wife for that year, and it's been such a wonderful year that I can only thank Him for it.

"And when He did take him Home to be with Himself, my heart was completely stayed upon the Lord. I was so thankful that in the past He has led me to trust Him for lesser things, that when this greater test came, I could trust Him completely. In so many ways the Father's hand was evident those last days that I can say, 'The Lord is kind in all His doings'. He seemed to separate us gently and made those last moments so precious to remember.

"And since then as I have read His Word, His precious promises for those who mourn and for the broken-hearted, and for those who feel their weakness and their need, have proved so very true, every one of them. So wonderful has been His comfort that in fact, today, I can look forward to the future, and accept His new plan for my life, as my whole life reaches out to Him in longing and desire to know Him better.

"I know that for Roy now is fullness of joy in the Saviour's presence. When I see the sun beating down, I think, 'I don't need to worry about Roy on the trail toiling up those steep hills with a heavy pack on his back.' Or else, when the rain comes down, think of the times when he used to be alone on the trail and many times up to his knees in mud and slipping down the hills. Now he is free from all this and it's joy, pure joy in His presence. In fact, sometimes as I go about my daily work, I feel that perhaps he is nearer than when he was away on the trails, for the Lord is with me, and Roy is with the Lord!

"Since then, the Lord has given me our little son, Murray Roy. He is growing so well, and when he is a few months older, I hope to take him back to the Meo tribe. The cost to make Christ known has been a life laid down—the dearest treasure He could ask of me. But He is worthy. I feel that there is a message the Lord would give to the Meo through me, by way of completing what He has done and is going to do through Roy.

"At the present time there are only two women missionaries left among the White Meo; but could God not answer our prayers through revived Meo Christians dedicated to Christ? Missionaries have laboured several years now among them and faithful prayer partners have shared the burden in a very real way. Roy and I have only entered into their labours this past year. But I wonder if Roy's life laid down might not be the *last link in the chain of God's purposes before the harvest.*"

Roy had confidently expected a great harvest among the Meo. Who was to take his place? God had not forgotten the burden of his heart for another man for the White Meo team. See a young man on his knees in deep soul struggle, conscious God was speaking to him about the Meo. It was Robin Talbot to whom Roy had poured out his heart three months earlier. He rose from his knees as the matter was cleared before the Lord, at 9 a.m. on May 16, just two hours before Roy was shot! Writing of his call, Robin recounted: "As for the present, Celia and I are longing to start in the Meo work. Never before have I had such a strong and urgent call from the Lord. For this my heart rejoices. . . . I know the battle ahead will be fierce and severe, and never have I felt so inadequate and weak to fill a gap, especially the gap left by Roy. My great comfort lies in God's power to turn weakness into His strength, and make a young lad's gift to feed a multitude. Our burden now is, 'O for a thousand Meo tongues to sing my great Redeemer's praise!' Celia and I are praying for many more prayer partners who will know how to pray, both when the Enemy comes in like a flood, and when the Holy Spirit of God is sweeping through the mountains in converting power."

The Meo were just beginning to plant their rice when Roy's life was taken. The rains had begun and the ground was soft for planting. It was then that Roy became that corn of wheat which, "if it dies . . . bear a rich harvest", John 12.24 (N.E.B.). Many Meo hearts had been made soft by Roy's fervent prayer and witness.

A few months later came the days of harvest. Days of sunshine in Meo-land ripened the heads of rice which had been watched with eager longing. Months of lean rice supply were over and the rice was being cut! Although it meant hard work from early dawn till late at night, yet there was a new spring in Meo steps. Oh, what joy! The harvest had begun!

So it was with the spiritual harvest. During the few months following Roy's death, twelve families in scattered Meo villages expressed their desire to follow Jesus and burn their demon paraphernalia. Was this by chance? No! It was the result of God's law of harvest. The prayed-for harvest was just beginning.

Gillian, with little Murray Roy, moved up to Palm Leaf, and with Dorothy Jones and Doris Whitelock sought to teach the new believers, many of whom were located in Bitter Bamboo. Roy had seen the beginning of revival in the Meo church. Now Ying, Simon, and other church leaders were displaying spiritual gifts and a new concern for the lost around them.

God was preparing several young men for a ministry among their own people. Don Rulison wrote after the 1964 Annual Believers Conference, "I specially recall Ying's morning message on the urgency of our commission to get the Gospel to the present generation as the multiplying grave markers on the mountain sides remind us of the brevity and immediacy of the present opportunity. Then, Simon's closing impassioned plea for everyone to be careful not to overlook that there were only two ways, and he most graphically set them forth to the tribes-men, using the Bible illustration of the rich man and Lazarus." Many were more prosperous through the marketing of vegetables which they had learned from Roy to produce. Simon's burden now was that no one should be complacent with material prosperity and mere profession while walking the road to hell. "I came away," Don continued, "feeling more strongly than ever the need of a leadership training school. They were ready for it!"

In the Big Mountain area Ying and Leah had the joy of seeing the first come to the Lord. On the mountain near Chiengmai where Roy and Gillian spent their honeymoon, there was not one believer in the several villages even after ten years' faithful witness, but a few months after Roy's death the first believers turned to Christ. In 1964 Don Rulison encouragingly reported, "They have increased ten-fold since last New Year, so we are praying for at least a similar increase before next year."

Thus the first two items of prayer covenant into which Roy entered with the Meo Team—the revival of the Meo church and a turning of the heathen to Christ—are beginning to be answered. *It is only a beginning.*

The third item of the prayer covenant—a spiritual quickening throughout the North Thailand field and the whole Mission—also shows encouraging signs of fulfilment. Roy's Thai teacher friend in his Chiengrai days, Jumrut, for whom Roy and his family had prayed regularly, came one day to the missionaries in the Chiengrai home. "Before, I was not ready," he said with lightened face, "but now I have fully accepted the Lord Jesus Christ with my whole heart."

He was baptized in Chiengrai on Sunday, May 19, 1963. As he came up out of the water, the missionary asked, "Do you know that just a year ago today Roy laid down his life?"

Jumrut smiled. "This is a fitting anniversary to my friend," he said softly.

Among the other tribes God is working. A missionary to the Yao writes, "Brother Six believes harvest time has come for the Yao tribe, and that thousands will become Christians. Already so many are burning their demon things that he can't respond to all the calls. The harvest truly is great, and we would urge your prayers that His great awakening will come to all the tribes."

Most thrilling of all has been the break in the Pwo Karen and the Lahu tribes where missionaries have worked for years without fruit. Now a missionary to the Lahu reports,

"Fittingly as to the season, the first-fruits of the Lahu tribe have been gathered in, for this is the very beginning of harvesting the early mountain rice. Are not first-fruits of a harvest an indication that there is much more ripened grain? Indeed, just at this time word has been sent out from one village to another, 'Let's *all* turn to the Lord now!'

"As the harvest of rice takes many hands and voices and long hours of diligent watching to chase away voracious birds that would spoil the harvest, we also need now many diligent watchers in prayer to stay the opposition to the ready harvest."

These are the beginnings. The promise of widespread blessing awaits spiritual fulfilment. Throughout the whole Mission is a deep and growing desire for a spiritual quickening in the whole of the Far East. New believers need to be taught and grounded in the Word of God. Who will teach them? Who will pray for them? Will some of the harvest be lost through lack of labourers?